Polishing th

Penelope Tarasuk

First published by Muswell Hill Press, London, 2017

www.muswellhillpress.co.uk.

British Library CIP Data available

ISBN: 978-1-908995-24-7

Printed in Great Britain

Permissions
Bergman, Ciel. (Cheryl Bowers) Painting: *Study for Her Sanctuary*. 1989. Author's private collection.

Symborska, Wislava. "Nothing's a Gift" from *View With a Grain of Sand: Selected Poems*. New York: Harcourt, Brace & Co., 1995. Used by permission, London, Faber and Faber Ltd. All rights reserved.

Whyte, David. "The Well of Grief" from *River Flow: New and Selected Poems*, ©2012, Many Rivers Press. Langley, WA. Used by permissions of Many Rivers Press. All rights reserved.

Polishing the Bones

Penelope A. Tarasuk, PhD, IAAP

Penelope Tarasuk's *Polishing the Bones is a poignant*, courageous, beautifully written story of psycho-spiritual healing and death/rebirth that transcends the boundaries and limitations of textbook therapeutic treatment and technique. With elegant prose and revelatory insight, Tarasuk shares her epic saga of a profound, deeply unique, therapeutic relationship, where she frees herself from the status quo and become a co-adventurer with the seeker. This shared adventure reveals to them both the far horizons of not only psycho-spiritual death/rebirth, but the radical healing potential of the actual death experience itself.

The story is a strikingly beautiful blueprint of the potentials inherent in an adventure where therapist and client both embark on a shared journey of transformation. A must read for all seekers and people-helpers willing to take the sacred leap of faith by trusting the infallible inner healing resources within the seeker herself.

Tav Sparks is the author of *The Power Within: Becoming, Being, and the Holotropic Paradigm* and is Director of Grof Transpersonal Training.

Dedicated

with love to Jesse and Gabe.
May this work support of the liberation of all sentient beings.

Nothing's A Gift

Nothing's a gift, it's all on loan.
I'm drowning in debts up to my ears.
I'll have to pay for myself
With myself,
Give up my life for my life.

Here's how it's arranged:
The heart can be repossessed,
The liver, too,
And each single finger and toe.

Too late to tear up the terms,
My debts will be repaid,
And I'll be fleeced,
Or, more precisely, flayed.

I move about the planet
In a crush of other debtors.
Some are saddled with the burden
of paying off their wings.

Others must, willy-nilly,
Account for every leaf.

Every tissue in us lies
On the debit side.

Not a tentacle or tendril
Is for keeps.

The inventory, infinitely detailed,
Implies we'll be left
Not just empty-handed
But handless, too.

I can't remember
Where, when, and why
I let someone open
Open this account in my name
We call the protest against this
The soul.
And it's the only item
Not included on the list.

Wislawa Symborska
View With a Grain of Sand: Selected Poems.

Contents

Acknowledgements

I would like to acknowledge and thank the many people who supported, guided, read, offered suggestions and encouraged me in the writing of this book: Marian Shapiro, Donna Graham, Rosemary Evans, Dale Schwarz, Nancy Riemer, Larry Peltz, Anita Greene, Thayer Greene, Soren Ekstrom, Carlyn Ekstrom, Jane Platko, Ira Sharkey, Maggie Bromell, Elizabeth Mayers, Kitty Moss, Karen Kleeman, Jane Carson, Elizabeth Martin, Pam Burnham, Barbara Burkart, Michael Burkhart, Betsy Crowell, Kathie Mc Quarrie, Susan Heath, Hillary Maddux, Diana Medina, Sophy Burnham, David Treadway, Nancy Mann, Carey Plitt, Eve Marko, Carol Rizzolo, Nina Friedman, Jonathan Roses, and Lorraine Roses.

Dr. Marion Woodman, elder Jungian wise woman, read my early manuscript and responded with enthusiasm, offered her wisdom, and encouraged me to publish; I thank you. Marian Shapiro, E.D.D. psychologist, author of Second Childhood, published poet, and classical musician, has been my steadfast and wise mentor. I deeply thank you for reading, witnessing, and encouraging me through this work from the beginning. I deeply respect and express gratitude for the Tibetan Buddhist Lamas and the wisdom teachings I've been offered over many years.

Mary (Crowell) Yost, NYC literary agent and advisor believed in this book and started me on the road to publishing. Janet Sadler edited an early draft. Jean Zimmer's expert editing near the end of the writing was extremely valuable.

I express gratitude for my writing mentor, prolific author, and friend, Linda McCulloch Moore. Your professionalism, support, wise guidance encouraged my words to become prayers that became stories. The Friday morning writing group: Maggie Bromell, Jean Z., Kathy, Missy, Gia, Eve, Dorothy, Claire, Jean B., and others; you have been immeasurably important and have nourished my soul over many years.

Dr. Prana Rose Meiss, Cell Biologist, retired NYU professor and researcher, mentored me in a form of Australian breath work that was based in indigenous, nature-based practices including learning from the intelligence of whales and dolphins. She deeply honored the wisdom of the body and the depth of the spiritual life.

I am deeply grateful to The New England Society of Jungian Analysts and the C. G. Jung Institute of Boston, Ltd., especially Dr. Soren Ekstrom, for support of my analytic education, teaching, service, and passion in the field of analytical psychology. To all my patients, I offer my heartfelt appreciation and respect for you and our work together.

Ciel Bergman, artist, feminist and ecologist, generously granted permission to use of one of her paintings for the cover of this book. Dr. Jay Dufrechou, writer, professor, and GTT colleague offered his kindness, trust, and generosity. I express my profound gratitude to Stan Grof, M.D. for his pioneering work in transpersonal psychology and Holotropic Breathwork. Tim Read, M.D., and publisher of Muswell Hill Press, please accept my thanks for your vision, dedication, and trust.

Kate Rindy, who supported and helped me in countless ways over the many years of this book's development; I thank you for your love and your belief in this work. Dr. Lou Levin and our sons Jesse Levin and Gabe Tarasuk-Levin supported my long education and work as a psychoanalyst, spiritual seeker, artist and writer. Your patience, curiosity, humor, intelligence, trust and love are precious gifts beyond measure.

Introduction

This narrative is based on a true story of a woman's journey into the depth of meaning of her life and into her untimely dying with the help of her dreams, her art, her husband, friends and a woman Jungian psychoanalyst.

This is the story of a long and deep psychological treatment I undertook with a middle-aged woman I call Laura, who was in many ways *every* woman. In her life she had many roles: mother, sister, daughter, wife, artist, muse, friend, partner, former wife, stepmother, employee, naturalist, activist, employee, employer, and student. Laura was my patient for nearly eight years, meeting many challenges, including profound illness, with creativity and grace. She died at age sixty-four following a life of emotional and mental openness, curiosity, and wonder.

We met consistently over seven years, both of us taking time away from her treatment for travel and family matters. I witnessed as Laura reported her dreams and began to experience the power and depth of symbols. Our roles reversed in the last three months as her life came to completion through a fateful illness. She became my teacher in dying and death. The continuous stream of dreams from her unconscious over seven years provided *aqua vitae*, the water of life, for her deep spiritual thirst. She willingly and honestly worked with life's challenges.

The psychological work with this patient over time was mutually deeply transformative. I feel that I became a more mature analyst and a more compassionate human being in this process. Laura died in a state of peace; I was present at her side. The following year I began writing as a creative way of reflecting on life and death, grieving, and honoring the relationship between us.

Although the heart of this story is inspired by true events, it is a story. Many details are changed, as are descriptions of people, places, dates, identities, events, and dialogue, in order to protect privacy, confidentiality, and anonymity. The essence of the story is preserved and Laura's dreams are presented as she reported them. She wanted me make use of her life story, dreams, and journals through writing and teaching for the purpose of helping others in their discovery of life's meaning, which might lead them to a greater sense of peace as they reach the completion of their lives. Laura and her husband gave me explicit permission.

Memory is imperfect and we each inevitably distort what we see and experience through our flawed human lens and personal complexes, no matter how well trained or well intended we may be. I ask that my readers accept the truth of these limitations. This story is communicated with compassion, sensitivity and every attempt at essential honesty.

Laura and her husband Eugene came from modest families and were encouraged to seek higher education. They had the good fortune of being physically attractive, socially at ease, intelligent, capable of humor, and highly verbal. People wanted to be around them. Like so many people; they personally and as a couple suffered different degrees of early emotional neglect and challenge, physical and medical limitations, personal disappointments, a range of traumas, and many emotional losses.

The couple had the capacity, discipline, and motivation to work long hours, the willingness to do research in attempts to solve challenging problems. They could ask for help, receive it and, were able to offer help to others. They were creative and worked as an effective team. The illusion of an "easy life" distorts the harsh realities and stresses that are a real part of such lives. Their work included many failures and disappointments. Their challenges and stubborn refusal to give up in the face of many disappointments fueled their success. Their curiosity, well-developed organizational skills, business acumen, foresight, and generosity with others served them well in their lives.

We cannot know what we will face in life or in dying. Each of us will use whatever resources we have, no matter how limited. We learn from Laura's story what is most important: that we each need present, compassionate human relationships to feel fully alive and, if possible, many of us want to be surrounded by compassionate relationships in our dying.

The story follows Laura's Jungian psychoanalysis in a linear form. The treatment follows her understanding in our initial phone conversation that I planned to relocate from Boston to Santa Fe, New Mexico. This would take place in several years. In this phone conversation she declined my referral to another colleague, a well-respected, highly experienced woman Jungian analyst. Laura made the decision to start with me. In anticipation of my future relocation we discussed a possible plan to continue therapy when that time came. At that time we discussed weekly telephone sessions and an intensive week of face-to-face meetings in Boston four times a year. After I moved, Laura would be invited to have sessions in person any time she traveled to Santa Fe. In the course of her therapy Laura recorded several hundred dreams in numerous journals. She loved to write, hand-wrote her dreams, and sent copies of over three hundred dreams that we worked with in treatment. Laura's analysis and dream work began prior to the explosion of email usage and our current collective dependence on communication technologies.

In this book I select a limited number of specific dreams to illustrate her response to the ongoing therapeutic work and as examples of expressions from her unconscious. The reader is invited into Laura's psychic process as well as my internal reflections. Throughout this narrative I share my thoughts, many of which were not spoken aloud to Laura during the analysis. I knew it was important for her to have her own bodily, mental, emotional experience, and associations during the sessions. I did share many thoughts and responses with her throughout the years. I suggested that she follow up some sessions by reading and researching books and articles to deepen her experience and knowledge of her symbolic material, and context of geography, historical events, creatures, and stories from many cultures. I strongly encouraged her to express her feelings through art, poetry, active imagination, and dance between our sessions. She followed these suggestions and encouragements with curiosity. She was a student of humanities, interested in a wide range of arts, ideas, science, environmental concerns, and politics. At a crucial point in her early treatment, approaching early childhood memories, Laura searched through many boxes shipped from her earlier home. The boxes had been stored unopened for years. She found the one containing her doll, handmade by her mother as well as all the doll's clothing her mother made. She washed and ironed each piece, taking time to remember and feel details of her early life. She brought the doll and clothing into her session literally and figuratively, unpacking emotional memories. This was a turning point in her as well as in our relationship; a tender, deep trust was being secured. She, like most children, stored and projected a great deal of her early emotional life onto a physical object, for Laura the object was her doll and the clothing.

Trusting the trajectory of her psyche and dreams, I followed her as she experienced and integrated psychological, emotional work. I was often amazed and humbled. My job was to listen closely and encourage her to delve deeper into feelings. The emergence of concerns that she had pushed out of consciousness due to shame and fear and the many distractions of life now had a safe space for expression. Work with "shadow" material is often felt as shameful to our ego consciousness and conflicts with the persona we present to the world. We all have "shadow" material in the unconscious in one form or another. I supported her creative expression and curiosity. She found teachers and learned new skills. Much later during her analysis she began to study ancient Greek.

Traditional Jungian analysis was the structure or form or 'frame' of our therapeutic work. Our analytic relationship was essential, the sacred vessel, or *temenos,* where transformation was underway.

What I didn't realize until later was how much I too was being transformed in and by the depth of this treatment and this relationship. We shared a positive transference and counter- transference that supported this long deep work. We shared an unnamed, unarticulated, experience of love. This was not an erotic or sexual transference; it was a gift in the realm of the heart, the soul, *agape.* Late in her therapeutic treatment, after extensive medical tests and biopsies, Laura was diagnosed with a terminal medical illness. The time came for the formal termination of our traditional Jungian analytic work.

Laura realized that the demands of her putting her life's affairs in order and anticipating increasing issues of physicality were radically changing. After reflection and discussion, she and her husband (whom I'd had no contact with in the previous seven years) called to ask if I would consider coming to help her, help them, during her dying. We entered into a different and very direct conversation. They relationship they proposed was a new role, a new configuration of tasks, and a new vessel or 'frame' of working together. Laura asked me directly to consider the possibility of helping her die. All would take place in their home. We made a formal, explicit business contract; I was paid for my work and they paid travel expenses. I was invited to live with them. I would be given a private room of my own and I would work as part of a circle of caregivers. I would come every other week, to live for a full week, through her death. In this story I speak in more depth about my experience of this transition into Laura's end of life, her dying, and death.

I take full responsibility for my thoughts, reflections, attempts to describe my way of analytic work and my behavioral decisions in the course of this treatment and the writing of this book. Although my psychotherapeutic and analytic education was traditional, my decision to accompany Laura and her family at the end of her life was unorthodox, not part of my Institute education or training and does not represent the attitudes, nor is it endorsed by the New England Society of Jungian Analysts and is not part the C. G. Jung Institute of Boston, Ltd. program of training and practice.

Contemplating Death and Dying

Dr. Elizabeth Kübler-Ross (1926-2004) was a Swiss psychiatrist working in the Department of Psychiatry at the University of Chicago in 1965. She was approached by four theology students at the Chicago Theological Seminary asking for her help with a research project on "crisis in human life." After discussions they agreed they that death was the biggest crisis that people faced. Traditional research parameters and data collection methods were intrusive at such a vulnerable time in a person's life. They decided upon a new approach: interviewing terminally ill patients and reversing traditional roles. The patients were to become their teachers. Kübler-Ross's first book, *On Death and Dying*[1] (1969), was based upon what they learned about patient's coping mechanisms at the time of a terminal illness. She wrote about the importance of the patient's feelings of isolation and fear and need for close human relationships, especially as time of dying approached. No one at the hospital seemed to have the specific role of speaking with the dying patients about their feelings and experience of the dying process. Patients in the study expressed gratitude for the presence of skilled listeners who had a willingness to talk about death and dying. From her observations, Kübler-Ross postulated four emotional stages of dying: denial, anger, depression, and resignation or acceptance. These stages were not seen as a direct or smooth process of moving forward, but rather as forward movement with times of regression. Each person has a unique form of expression and timing in the dying process.

I attended one of Kübler-Ross's public talks on death and dying in 1974 in Washington, D.C. At the time I was finishing graduate school and planning to move to Boston to work. I listened to a surprisingly small, bird-like woman, wearing glasses, speaking with a heavy German accent. She reviewed much of what was in her 1969 book and spoke about "Hospice," an organization begun by an English woman physician, Dame Cecily Saunders, M.D., O.B.E., author of *Care of the Dying*[2] (1989). I'd never heard of Hospice. After the talk I approached Dr. Kübler-Ross to thank her for the presentation and her work on behalf of so many. I remember feeling her delicate bones in that handshake. She had set out to change this country's attitudes and behavior toward death and dying and was speaking for thousands of patients who had no voice or were too compromised to talk or fight for more humane care. Deeply impressed by this very small, powerfully articulate woman of conviction, I wanted to know more. After settling in Boston I wrote to her, asking where I could further study the subject of death and dying. She promptly wrote back a personal letter suggesting that I meet with her colleagues at the Massachusetts General Hospital Department of Psychiatry and Reverend Dr. Mwalimu Imara. He was teaching at Boston University and acting as the minister of the Arlington Street Church in Boston. His work with the terminally ill began when he was Kübler-Ross's assistant and colleague in her initial death and dying seminars at the University of Chicago. I contacted Reverend Dr. Imara and, with his mentor's referral, was immediately invited to join his class. The small group seminar met one evening a week for several months. Each member of the group was asked to contemplate their own dying, death, and the deaths of beloved family members. I was twenty-seven years old.

It was the first time that I'd thought with any depth and maturity about my own death and mortality. I'd formerly thought about being killed, being in accidents, but I'd never consciously reflected on a slow, considered dying process, especially after a long life. I hadn't thought much about my own aging. But there I did. In this group I imagined myself into the future, becoming very old. I had the sensation that I was literally drying up and then the wind blew me away like late autumn leaves. It was so natural. Although I had been present at the deaths of animals and had known of deaths, now I realized that *my* dying would happen and that death is like birth, simply a part of our nature, our human condition. We were asked to contemplate our funeral or memorial services. The profundity of this course was daunting, humbling, and humanizing. There was no distancing or intellectualizing through books and talks. Dr. Imara opened us to another level of reality. He asked us to dwell upon what was formerly unimaginable. With his help I was able to think about and imagine death.

The subtle and unconscious psychological defense of "denial" of death is very powerful. Earnest Becker (1924-1974) received the Pulitzer Prize for his book, *The Denial of Death* [3](1973). He delved into the psychological defense of denial of death and discussed his understanding and philosophy of life.

Death and dying swiftly dropped into my unconscious as I immersed my young adult life in love and work, ego and personality development, homemaking, art, meditation, two pregnancies and births, raising a family, and my Jungian psychoanalytic training. It was the time of establishing and belonging to communities. Occasionally realizations about death returned to my consciousness, such as during my natural childbirths labor and when medical test results were alarming. I had the luxury and blessing that no one close to me emotionally died during these years. When someone else's death "happened" I unconsciously avoided deep reflection. Unless death was personal, very close, it was easier to deny.

The Education of a Jungian Psychoanalyst

The word "psychoanalyst" is used as a general descriptive term in this story. A Jungian psychoanalysis contains the meaning and practices of psychotherapy and includes a wide range of depth psychologies and dream work. All Jungian psychoanalysts develop *first* through the work of preparing to be a psychotherapist in its true ancient Greek meaning: the attendants who served the god by carrying out the prescribed ritual, "*therapeute*s." C. A. Meier, author of *Ancient Incubation and Modern Psychotherapy*[4] states, "… The most famous physician of late antiquity was Galen (131 A.D.- 201 A.D.) who styled himself the *therapeut* of his fatherly god, Asclepius." The divine physician healer had appeared to Galen in a dream. In antiquity everything to do with the psyche (soul) was embedded in religion. We could say that Asclepius carries or evokes the archetype of a divine physician/healer, the one who tends of the body and soul, and one who invites the patient to seek healing dreams. Through our dreams the process of inner healing can be expressed. Healing does not necessarily mean curing an illness in the physical body. Healing is related to creating a meaningful life, a life that strives toward greater wholeness that includes death, a life that values relatedness and compassion.

Throughout this story I choose to use the descriptive word "patient" instead of the word "client". I find that most people come into therapeutic treatment because they are in pain, suffering bodily, emotionally, and in soul. I find that the word "client" has an association or feel of business and commerce exchange in the material world. Indeed, there is a business, financial aspect and exchange that must be dealt with professionally, realistically, and responsibly. I find that the real meaning in analytic or depth psychotherapy is the work with dis-ease in the emotional, mental, social, and spiritual life of the patient.

Becoming an analyst is a lengthily and deeply meaningful commitment of postgraduate (M.D., M.A., M.S.W., Ph.D., Psy.D., E.D.D.) studies. I entered my analytic training at the fledgling C. G. Jung Institute of Boston in the spring of 1979. One of the first four students, I was the only woman and newly pregnant with my first son. I received my Diploma in Jungian Analysis in 1988, mother of two sons. I took brief leaves of absence around the time of my children's births and was fortunate to have and continue a private practice in a renovated carriage house separate from our home. My husband, a child psychologist, was a wonderful father and a supportive partner. As demanding as it was in those early years, I found that giving birth naturally, nursing, attaching, and creating a secure holding environment for my sons helped me to understand and embody the many of concepts and theories I was studying intellectually.

Like medical surgeons or other specialists, analysts in training devote many years of study under the tutelage of experienced colleagues who've practiced this art and science for many years. To enter the profession of a Jungian analyst one usually feels a calling or a sense of "vocation." It is work in psychology and psychotherapy with a spiritual core. My professional life in human service developed over many years, before I even considered psychoanalytic education. By 1975 when I began a Jungian analysis I had already experienced years of psychotherapy for myself. I had worked for thirteen years as a psychotherapist in many settings: inpatient and outpatient and with people of many races, cultures, and classes. It is a long road to develop the abilities and to earn the privilege to practice and work with such deep intimacy. In this field, we analysts, *unlike* surgeons and many other specialists, must commit to work on our own psychic sufferings and patterns of behavior prior to and during training. We are required to deeply examine our lives in our own treatment with more experienced colleagues before and during treatment of patients. Jungian analytic studies include psychological theories of human development and a variety of treatment modalities, world religions and spiritual practices, anthropology and cultural studies, world mythologies, fairy tales, and folklore. We study psychiatry, psychopathology, basic psychopharmacology, ethics, qualitative research, and clinical research in neurobiology and the developing brain. We study contemporary issues such as violence in society, war, international terrorism, contemporary issues of use and effects of technology in human development and the use of technology and media in analytic practice. The consequences of poverty, domestic violence, rape, legal and illegal immigration concerns, the long shadow of racism, public health, economics, gender expression and inequality, and world politics are part of our analytic education and the analytic society's discussions. Patients are aware of and affected by these issues and events and often bring dreams about these subjects into their treatment. What we cannot cover in seminars we are encouraged to research and make use the broad array of educational resources and opportunities in our urban area.

My Personal Introduction to the Psychology of Carl Jung

I was introduced to the work of Dr. Carl Gustav Jung in my early child-hood. He was a Swiss medical doctor and psychiatrist (1875-1961) who lived during a time of the emergence great interest in the unconscious, the psyche. Deeply influenced by his senior mentor, Dr. Sigmund Freud, Jung was interested in the conscious aspects of psyche and the effects of the unconscious on consciousness. He felt that the meaning of life was motivated by a spiritual source of life, not solely through instinctual drives; he developed a theory of archetypal psychology. He explored the depths of his own unconscious, most notably illustrated in his personal journal, The Red Book[5] published in 2009. His study of spirituality, world religions, mythology and anthropology informed his thinking and theories. He is well known for his deep interest in dreams and non-ordinary experiences including archetypal states of mystery, numinosity, and synchronicity.

In my childhood, between the ages of four to eight, my father was in therapy for posttraumatic stress disorder (PTSD) related to his World War II experiences as a U.S. Navy diver. He had been part of team of highly experienced deep-sea divers who were assembled and brought to Pearl Harbor, Hawaii immediately after the bombings, December 1941. He descended repeatedly into the sunken, catastrophically ex-ploded and tangled battleships in attempts to save many endangered lives and to retrieve the dead bodies of hundreds of lost servicemen.

The trauma of his terrifying and profoundly dangerous Navy expe-riences evoked, or triggered, emotionally overwhelming memories of losses of family members and his own traumatic experiences in child-hood. The Veterans Administration of the U.S. sent a psychologist, Dr. Gordon Tice, to my grandmother's home in Washington, D.C. where my family was living. I remember this psychologist as a kind, tall man with gold-rimmed glasses. He was a psychotherapist who de-scribed himself as a "Jungian", someone deeply influenced by the ideas of Carl Jung, M.D., and he was a Unitarian minister. Dr. Tice and my father sat in our open living room during their weekly meetings. Curi-ous and concerned, I was sometimes allowed to sit nearby on the floor. They discussed many things including the works of Freud, Jung, Greek philosophers Aristotle, Socrates, and Plato, and world religions. My father spoke of his experiences of war, his personal history, and the human condition. Dr. Tice encouraged him to paint pictures, carve stat-ues, and write stories. I remember my father carving a wooden statue of a whale and painting: it was Moby Dick and a tiny wooden rowboat with oars set in turbulent ocean. After home-based psychotherapeutic treatment was terminated, my father and Dr. Tice exchanged meaningful, and deeply cherished correspondence regularly for thirty-five years, until my father's death.

My father developed a library of books on many psychological subjects including books on existential psychology and the history of World War II. I looked at books on the Holocaust illustrated with numerous official photographs. I couldn't comprehend the idea or reality of holocaust or death but I was aware of terror and suffering. The seeds of my interest in the arts, philosophy, spirituality, psychology, and the human condition including good and evil took root very early, shaping my life and vocation. The suffering of my family and humanity was not veiled in my early life. My father experienced "the dark night of his soul", a psychotic descent into his unconscious, and, fortunately, and with skilled help, he emerged a more whole, more psychologically integrated person able to resume a productive life in our family and society.

PART-I

Know Thyself

Spoken by the Oracle of the Greek god Apollo and engraved in the forecourt of Apollo's Temple in Delphi, Greece. These ancient words are replete with meaning, and are the touchstone for many philosophers. This powerful instruction continues through time in spiritual traditions, the arts, and depth psychology, especially the analytical and archetypal psychology of Dr. Carl Gustav. Jung.

CHAPTER 1

The Last Dance

I am at Laura's home near the Green Mountains of Vermont.

It is dawn, the last morning that Laura walks. She will die soon. This is the moment when she voluntarily falls to her knees, and in this moment she has a vision of a deer.

In her tiny bathroom with a knotty-pine Dutch door, just seventeen slow steps from her recently arranged bedroom on the first floor, in this, Laura calculates by the hour her body's withdrawal from this world. With the mind of a chemist she uses a measuring cup to calculate the amount of fluids taken in and going out. She is not giving up hope. She glances up through the window toward the mountains freshly covered in snow. She calls me into the bathroom near her. In this moment she voluntarily drops to her knees: she whispers her vision, her epiphany.

> *"Oh! I see the deer!*
> *It is breaking through the snow and ice and is drinking deeply from the cold water!"*

The approach of the vision is swift, quiet, and filled with awesome beauty. A fleeting gentle creature of the earth and wind, the deer is sacred in many ancient cultures. I know that Laura has been unable to eat or drink for days; she is starving, dehydrated, medicated, and is dying. Only Laura, who cherished nature and wild animals, can see this deer and river. This creature with its beauty and swiftness is precious to Laura. The ancient ones said that the deer is a herald of death.

Suddenly, in complete openness, she is passionately praying aloud for the earth and the rivers, for all lives, and the planet's well being. Feeling awe, I quietly stay near her witnessing and hearing her whole-hearted prayer.

Her physical strength gone now, Laura can no longer stand. Gentle night-helper Jamie and I are unable to lift her, fearing we might hurt her swollen, fluid-filled belly. Jamie summons her husband Eugene from his brief sleep in the living room. Sleepily, he comes to tenderly lift her.

She rises slowly in his arms, standing on his feet. Here, in a dreamy dawn world, he, a knight in his pale blue bathrobe and she, his lady in her oversized silk pajama bottoms and cotton top, slowly move together across the room swaying, humming, and dancing. They dance regally to Laura's bed, where she comes to rest for her final hours of labor and liberation. I am watching the utter sweetness possible in human relationship. Here at this fragile tender time of great transition is the fruit of nearly three decades of relationship, "the last dance".

Standing near, I am witnessing and remembering simultaneously part of a dream that Laura had shared with me nearly eight years ago at the beginning of her Jungian analysis:

Dream: I am looking for a dance partner...

Laura has danced her life.

Those of us who know her are forever blessed by moments such as this.

CHAPTER 2

Laura Calls

Beginning.

One afternoon in late summer I receive a telephone call.

I am working in my garden and come in to answer the phone.

"Hello, how may I help you?"

"Hello. My name is Laura. A dear friend, a therapist in California who knows about Jung's psychology, referred me to you. I'd like to come to see you for treatment. I have been thinking about this and reading some of Jung's work over these last few years."

Her voice is soft and gentle with clear articulation. I understand that this referral was made with the personal care of a close friend and carries a kind of blessing or hope. I understand this from my own experience, that when psychoanalysts, psychotherapists, psychiatrists and doctors refer their own close friends or family to another similar professional they hope for the best care and a good fit in relationship.

"What are your concerns, what brings you to this decision?" I ask.

"If I were to state it succinctly, it would be a broken-heart," she says. We speak briefly about her life concerns as a middle-aged woman and arrange a time to meet in my home office outside of Boston.

I live in a quiet, old neighborhood of Victorian era homes near Tufts University, a few miles North of Boston. My office, once a carriage house, is a separate building. The space is simple and open with large windows, oak floors, a cathedral ceiling, skylights, and a very old Chinese rug. The rug is bordered in deep blue, the background a deep rust color with a gold center. Birds of paradise with long tail feathers hold flower baskets in each of the four corners. It belonged to my Irish grandmother and was in her Washington D. C. home. This rug was a magic carpet for me in my early childhood during very difficult years. The rug has traveled with me throughout my life and services as a reminder of support, survival, ancient cultures, art, and the power of imagination.

The office is furnished simply with a large comfortable light-blue couch, my wooden rocking chair, an antique oak secretary desk, stored here for a friend, and two full bookshelves. French doors open onto a very small yard and garden with a pink dogwood tree that blooms profusely in late April. Light enters the room from four directions.

For me, meeting every new patient is a conscious step into the unknown. At a profoundly deep level, it is similar – a sliver of similarity – to a mother meeting her newborn. I feel anticipation and curiosity, forgetting all the hard work to come.

I always experience this first meeting as a fateful encounter. It is always my hope that this relationship will become life changing or at least life enhancing for us both.

Although I tell Laura that I will be relocating to the Southwest in several years, my more immediate concern is her commute to my office from her home in Vermont, a significant trip: six-hours round trip by car at least once weekly.

She is undaunted by both concerns. "I am ready to meet next week. I want to begin."

Laura arrives promptly for our first meeting, her first session. She has no trouble with my directions. Laura is remarkable in her willingness to make a significant effort to travel so far to see me. She seems in many ways quite familiar to me, and as a new patient, she is simply a person seeking help with her life.

She is emotionally warm, physically fit, and of medium stature. She is perhaps five foot three inches tall and has grace about her. Laura has a small build, good posture. She offers a beautiful soft smile and looks directly at me with clear bright eyes. After we exchange a greeting with our eyes and a soft handshake, she sits on the couch near my chair. She seems at ease with me, interested and curious.

Middle-aged, she is dressed in soft earth-toned clothing, no jewelry, no makeup. Her medium-length brown hair is brushed and held back simply. She is not at all glamorous. She presents herself with a quiet beauty and natural elegance. It is easy for me to like her immediately. Settling into the couch, her hands move to her lap, her eyes cast downward; she takes a breath as if she is gathering within before starting something important.

Her story begins.

"I spent a lot of time in boarding schools beginning at age six and all the way through high school. There were certainly many advantages to such communal life in beautiful country settings. It began with my mother's teaching at a school when I was about five. We had financial needs. Mother needed to make a living during the war and I could attend the schools for almost no cost", Laura hesitates then says, "Perhaps my living with my mother at boarding schools made up for not having much of a home life in my early years."

I already feel a sense of tragic loss. She takes time to breathe; her hands are very still in her lap, her eyes still downcast. She tells me that she had very recent experience that prompted her to make the call, to seek help. The actual immediate event that triggered her was a phone call from a man she had not heard from in many years.

She begins to cry softly. "Alex was my first real boyfriend, my first love. He was a transfer student, born in Germany. He graduated from the same boarding school several years ahead of me. We wanted to marry." Laura looks up and away and continues, "He lived near Dresden during World War II. Toward the end of the war American bombers targeted his city. He and his mother suffered the horror and chaos of the bombing of their city including their home. He survived the bombing; his mother did not. His father was lost earlier." Laura covers her eyes, then sighs, "He told me stories of living in a war zone and described crawling out of the rubble that had been his home."

She tells me that he was sent to America by concerned relatives. They wanted him to complete his education and it wasn't safe living in Germany. They were able to secure a place for him at the boarding school. She and Alex shared a love of nature and learning. They fell deeply in love. She continued, "I was so young, completely innocent. After graduating from high school he left, returning to his relatives in Germany. The war was over."

Laura's father was an only child, the son of German immigrants. They were Christian. He was educated as a civil engineer and business administrator. He refused to allow her to follow Alex to Germany and wouldn't give his permission for her to marry him. She never forgot her father's firm refusal of her wishes. "He told me that my Alex was too old for me, I was much too young to marry, and that Alex would want to live in Germany. My father wouldn't allow it. His words were final. I was obedient to my father's authority."

Crying quietly, Laura lifts her head and says, "My life's course was altered. I lost the young man I loved. At that time in my life I had only begun to understand the trauma and collateral damage of war, the imprisonments, killings and torture of innocent civilians." Laura turns her head from side to side, "I was so ashamed of myself, disappointed that I backed down, surrendered to my father's demands."

The lives of Laura and Alex followed different paths. Beginning in her last year of high school she began a deeper study of history and began to contemplate the meaning of war. She felt the need to know about the Holocaust. She graduated from high school quietly depressed and bearing a broken heart over the loss of Alex. She then reveals to me that she kept a sporadic correspondence over decades with Alex after they separated.

As Laura speaks, I am reminded of the patients I have worked with over the years who attended boarding schools. Few did so this early in life or for this length of time. All these patients discuss disrupted family experiences and longing for an intimate nuclear family. What are the consequences for Laura?

"I began at Barnard, a women's college in New York City, on a full scholarship," Laura continues. She says that her father wanted her to live at home, go to a state school, and become a teacher. The only reason she could go to Barnard was because of this scholarship. After just one year she withdrew to get married. In reflection, she is sure there was some desperation in her decision. Marriage, early marriage, was what so many people did in that time, the 1950s. She says, "I truly regret my decision to leave college and get married so soon."

Laura relates that after the loss of Alex, she was very sad and longed for love and a family. Nick, who became her new husband, had also graduated from high school a year ahead of her. She met him in New York while socializing with college friends. Dating him, Laura found a new sense of life and of a future stirring. Nick had a way of gathering interesting people for enjoying music and rich conversations. Laura, emotionally vulnerable, immature and naïve found Nick irresistible. "He was so exciting, so handsome and charming He was a Princeton student with a beautiful mind, and he was in love with me. He had me in the palm of his hand." He proposed and her parents supported her decision to marry Nick.

After her brief college experience and her marriage, Laura stayed in New York City and found work in textile design. "At this time my mother died suddenly of a stroke. I was twenty. There was no funeral service. The following year I miscarried in the fifth month of my first pregnancy. I was alone. Nick was away. My family was away. Everyone was away." For Laura it was a shocking, bloody, frightening event. Shortly after the death of Laura's mother, her father remarried. His new wife had been his long-time secretary.

In describing her first marriage, Laura says she became deeply disappointed as time went on. At first the young couple shared Nick's parents' apartment. Before the marriage Nick had barely finished college. He had skipped many classes, preferring to write and socialize. School was less important than his plans for and dreams of becoming a writer.

"We lived an unconventional lifestyle with social gatherings for discussions of politics and art," Laura says, sighing. "Nick and his friends were passionate, exciting people." She adds that Nick's paid work was infrequent. Laura and his parents supported him.

In her second pregnancy Laura reluctantly agreed with her doctor to take medication to prevent another miscarriage. She read about birthing and came across the Lamaze method of natural labor and delivery. This breathing method allowed a woman greater involvement in the birth experience. "I sought and found a doctor in New York City who would allow natural childbirth which wasn't common, especially in cities like New York." At the time she had been concerned about the medication she ingested during the pregnancy, but received little support or interest in this issue from relatives or friends. She expressed lingering questions about the effect of the medication upon her pregnancy.

"The birth wonderful," Laura says. "I was awake. I felt such joy." Nick was not with her at the birth. Few men entered the delivery rooms of the hospitals at that time.

She had wanted to nurse her baby girl, "Karen" although her mother-in-law discouraged her. The apartment was cramped. Her mother-in-law was very emotionally involved and physically intrusive in the small apartment. "I had no real privacy," Laura sighs. "It's as if she wanted to take my baby away from me." Her mother-in-law competed with her for the baby's care. Laura managed, with little privacy, to nurse her baby for a few months.

Soon after, Laura returned to work. She helped with housework and cooking for the family. Occasionally she took her baby to work and remembers Karen cradled on her lap as she worked designing textiles. At the apartment Nick and his parents were frequently entertaining numerous friends. Laura enjoyed the company but could have used more physical help shopping, carrying groceries up the stairs, preparing meals, cleaning up and doing the laundry. Hospitality was very important to her and with so little support in those years, she eventually became exhausted.

CHAPTER 3

The Analysis Begins

Laura and Nick's decision to move to California was centered on Nick's goal to be a writer. He hoped that his parents' social and political connections would be helpful. After being blacklisted in the McCarthy era, along with many people in politics, her in-laws still found work difficult to come by. Laura says, "I was game, curious about California's progressive politics and the writing community."

She, Nick, Karen, now a toddler, and Nick's parents moved from New York City to California, initially renting a house all together near Palo Alto, not far from Stanford University. Laura found freelance design work and continued to support the family. Her husband and his friends were trying to break into the field of science writing. Very little money was coming in from his freelance work. Laura became pregnant again.

"I wanted to have more children and was happy to be pregnant. This time I refused medication to prevent miscarriage. The pregnancy and birth went well and my baby was healthy. He was such a beautiful baby boy, "Mark". Our home was crowded and our schedules chaotic. Finally, Nick's parents moved out. I felt such relief."

Laura took her two very young children to Ohio meet their grandfather and stepmother. She says, "They hadn't made the trip to see us yet. I am very glad I took my babies."

Not long after the visit, Laura received a telephone call from Jacqueline, her father's second wife who had been his secretary for years. Her father had died suddenly, unexpectedly suffering a massive heart attack. For Laura in her early twenties, this was another shocking, traumatic loss of a parent.

"Jacquie invited me to visit her in Ohio. There was to be no formal service or funeral for my father. I liked Jacquie when she was my father's secretary and I still do. At some point later I realized that it was likely that they were having an affair for many years during my parents' marriage. At first I was really distressed with this realization but it helped me to understand my mother's rages, her deep sadness, and loneliness. All these moods and behaviors were probably related to this. It wasn't just my father's extensive work away from home."

This memory led Laura to another memory of loss, "When I was seven my brother George, who was twelve years older than me and my only sibling, was away finishing college in Chicago. This was when Nonny, my beloved maternal grandmother, died. She had lived with us when I was very young. She was my hero and the first real artist I knew. She encouraged me in my artwork. She was wonderfully lively. I was told she a very "independent thinker". Nonny divorced her husband during the Great Depression after he forbade her to become an artist. She left him, traveled alone to the Southwest, and became a painter. I never knew my maternal grandfather. Nonny later returned to help my mother when I was a baby. She cared for me when I was three years old when my mother was hospitalized for some time. Later I learned that my mother's hospitalization was for a "nervous condition."

There was no funeral or memorial service for Laura's beloved grandmother.

Not long after her own father's death, Laura discovered that her husband, who had been staying home to care for the children while Laura worked at a design studio, was having an affair with her close friend. "The affair was going on while I was working. I felt shocked and betrayed by both of them," she says. Her hands come up, covering her mouth, "I was enraged!"

Making mental notes to myself, I reflect that by age three Laura had suffered a maternal separation of weeks or possibly months, due to her mother's depression; by age six she had lost the security of her nuclear family with her father's work often far from home, and her only sibling was considerably older and living away. Laura had gone with her mother to live at a boarding school. At age seven her beloved grandmother died. In her adolescence she lost her first love. She left college after just one year and was married at age nineteen. Not long after this her mother died suddenly and Laura's first pregnancy ended in a miscarriage. Her in-laws' support was ambivalent, complicated and problematic. She realized her father had an affair with his secretary, who became her stepmother. She experienced the second sudden death of a parent, her father. She was abruptly orphaned while raising two small children and supporting an unfaithful husband.

Her parents, and grandmother were the family members who were the most important people in Laura's early life. They were the ones she depended on for safety and love.

During these losses and her husband's betrayal, there was no time, place, or emotional space for her grief. There were no gatherings of the extended family or friends for her emotional support. As I listened, I perceived that Laura's in-laws and the circle of friends that she and Nick had developed were quite egocentric, narcissistic people. She really had no functional community to engage in or to support her.

I also wrote a note to myself about the importance of the fact that Laura did not have an emotional breakdown. This was highly significant, unlike her mother who had required hospitalization for a "nervous breakdown", Laura did not "breakdown". I perceived strength in Laura's psychic constitution. I wondered how she coped, in what ways she sustained her balance with such chronic traumatic losses. I know from many years of experience that there is always a steep emotional and physical price for chronic trauma and loss.

"Even before I knew about Nick's affair," Laura continues, "I was becoming increasingly fatigued and eventually went to a doctor. I was working and had young children but the fatigue was too deep for my age. The doctor ran tests; I was diagnosed with breast cancer. Here I was in my mid-twenties with two young children and almost no support, receiving such horrible news! I was immediately scheduled for surgery: a radical mastectomy, to be followed by radiation treatment. At that time, in the early 1960s, cobalt radiation was used. That treatment required that I be kept in isolation. My mother-in-law took over the care of the children. I was in the hospital for weeks and missed my children terribly. I knew it was dreadful for them, for us, to be separated for so long. Even when visiting was permitted, Nick refused to bring them to see me. While I was in the hospital recovering from surgery he let me know that he and his mother had given away the family dog. I fully realized this marriage wasn't working."

Laura returned home from the hospital devastated physically and emotionally. Her deep fatigue continued in the following weeks. Returning to her physician, further tests were run. She was then diagnosed with hepatitis B and C. It was determined that the hospital had accidently infected her with a contaminated blood transfusion during the surgery. In those years there was not adequate blood screening.

Weeks of slow recovery followed. Her brother George came to help her. Laura went on living with what she didn't know was a liver damaging, life threatening condition. During this time of acute illness and recovery Laura says she finalized the emotional fallout and made the decision to divorce her husband. She would use what small amount of money remained from a very modest life insurance policy left by her father. She left Nick and took the children to live in a small rented bungalow not far from the ocean. She describes this time alone with her young children as "perhaps one of the happiest times in my life."

She took Karen and Mark to the beach daily, made new friends with other young mothers, and was fortunately able to continue to work as a freelance designer. She took a few short-term jobs as a project assistant on documentary films. A skilled researcher, she also had an eye for set design. She had worked in fabric and textile design and now wanted to try costume design. It was her dream work, "a passion of mine since childhood," she says. She took jobs as a project assistant on documentary films to help meet expenses as a single mother. Various company executives attempted to extricate sexual favors from her in exchange for freelance work. "I refused!" There was one man, Gregory, who, Laura described as special, kind to her, and wonderful with the children. They dated and he helped to restore some of her confidence in her body and femininity. After the loss of her breast and the extensive scarring from the mastectomy Laura says quietly, "I felt such shame about the loss of my breast." This was before reconstructive surgery was suggested or common. "Gregory wanted to marry me and, although I did care for him and was grateful, I declined." Her textile and design work was successful and she was contemplating a job offer in Hawaii. At that time she received a call from a man who needed an assistant for a science documentary. He had heard about Laura's work on other projects. She went for an interview.

At this point in the session she decides to stop discussing past history and shifts to her more contemporary life circumstances. I feel that perhaps this was all she could share with me of her painful early history? It is the first, extended, session.

Laura shifts on the couch and takes a deep breath before she continues, "That was over thirty years ago." Eugene was the scientist who called her for the interview. Laura says, "He and I really hit it off immediately. Soon we were swept away with each other. He was an amazingly confident man and he admired my talents. He was honest about his difficulties, both financial and marital. I knew Gene was facing large debts and complicated divorce." He had two young children in his first marriage and Laura had her own divorce problems. She smiles, "We went ahead anyway and married in the whirl of happy chaos. We were young and fearless. We had very little money or property, but we had enthusiasm, drive, and love!" Laura describes Eugene as a gifted scientist with a open heart and mind and deep appreciation of the arts. He was becoming recognized in his field. Laura reminisces: "He hired me as an assistant on the documentary project he was making for NASA (National Aeronautics and Space Administration). We worked so well together. We were a dynamic team. It was California in the 60s and anything seemed possible."

Laura appears wistful as she considers how to describe the next years, "So much happened in those years. Those times were both good and bad for our family. There were many people in and out of our lives, some famous, and some real characters. We attended many art shows, science lectures, exhibitions, and learned about space programs. Our lives and work revolved around meetings. Always, there were meetings. Creative meetings, budget meetings, crisis meetings. Endless projects required endless meetings. It never stopped."

Laura slows down and her mood changes. "During this exciting and hectic time there was a frightening tragedy when my children were teens. In our neighborhood, two blocks away, there was a brutal murder of a family we'd known. Drug addicts high on methamphetamines broke into the neighbor's house. They probably were looking to steal money for more drugs, but found the family there. Those innocent people were viciously murdered." Laura is silent.

After a minute she goes on. "Karen and Mark had more unsupervised time in those years than I'd wished. They were resourceful kids but I know that not everything that happened to them, around them, was for the best. Eugene and I worked ceaselessly in our creative work. We did so much together and ..."

She is telling me that she feels guilty, without using that word, for not being with and not protecting her children. She accepted Eugene's limitations as a stepfather. Work came first for him, family and parenting were second. She couldn't rely on her former husband, Nick, to help raise the children. His inconsistent contact with them created additional problems; the now adolescent children were angry and confused. This anger was displaced onto her and Eugene. Karen and Mark began acting out–skipping school and hanging out with some unsavory characters.

Laura is describing her very lonely journey as a remarried mother without grandparents to help, without extended family support, and without strong, consistent fathering for her children, and all the issues and additional stress of a blended family.

The time for our first session is almost over. Laura shifts to the edge of the couch while looking at the clock. We had scheduled two hours for this initial session. I am aware that we have traveled far from the initial subject of "her lost love: Alex," who was the trigger for her call requesting treatment.

Laura attention turns back into the present time describing how Eugene has met with success from his many years of hard work. He currently has many business demands and creative science projects underway. Many of which take him away from home. "He travels frequently and is often away for weeks on end. I go with him some-times." Recently she joined him on a business trip to Japan. She smiles while describing Japanese country inns and exploring many art and craft studios. "Having this time to explore was unusual for us during business travel. This trip to Japan was especially meaningful to me. I enjoyed the arts, culture, and people." She then says, "Now I am find-ing that travel appeals less to me. Gene is preoccupied and emotionally unavailable on the trips. I want to be at home, in my garden, or reading and having a quieter life."

Laura, as with all my patients, dips in and out of memories and incidents and feelings. A life story is rarely related in a straightforward way, it never unfolds neatly. History-taking for me is an ongoing proj-ect like archeology, with layers and bits unearthed slowly over time. I am listening and observing intently to how Laura speaks, her choice of words, her body language, what she says and what she leaves out, what evokes great feeling in her and what she skirts over breezily. I listen for the places where there is an abrupt change of subject. Is this because there is too much discomfort or pain with the subject? Eventually I will ask her more about this as it is happening in the moment.

I know that anyone who begins psychotherapy or analysis in mid-life comes with quite a life story: numerous complicated relationships, many unfinished plans, and so much life to review. Like many people, Laura traveled, experienced living in several communities, and, made moves across the country. There are various chapters in all of our lives. These "chapters" are usually described, or centered in *relationships* with our most important loves. We all experience personal losses of people, with the places lived, and with our accomplishments or our failures.

Sometimes we know we are standing at a crossroad, at a major de-cision-making time in the path, or trajectory, of life. As I listen to Laura I feel she is at such a crossroad, and I believe she may know this too.

As this first session is coming to an end I note that Laura had be-come increasingly tired and less animated. Her posture is less upright, she is now sighing deeply, leaning forward and holding her face in her hands with her head bowed.

I say, "Both your parents both died suddenly, separately, many years ago. You lost your grandmother, your heroine. You never got to say good-bye. Those deaths were not observed with care. You gave birth to two babies and lost a pregnancy, all within a difficult first marriage. You suffered catastrophic health crises. Your very small extended family was barely engaged then and that continues now. Your children are grown and far away. Your husband is invested in an endless stream of creative projects requiring much of his time and attention away."

As I continue reflecting with Laura on the themes of loss she is describing, she begins to weep deeply, her body shuddering. This extended initial interview is unveiling the series of chronic, complex traumatic losses. We sit until she comes to the end of her tears.

Laura's initial presenting problem of a "broken heart" and depression was an expression of her many losses. The timely trigger of Alex's phone call unexpectedly serves as a path leading to her associated memories of her aching and broken heart through these multiple losses. She had already been thinking about beginning treatment. Her accompanying symptoms of depression with frequent bouts of sadness and crying, literal pain in her heart, difficulty sleeping, and loneliness are symptoms communicating her unresolved, not fully experienced, grief. I hear her search for intimacy, her emotional and physical fatigue, and other things left unsaid at this time. Her animated persona of "lovely delight and simplicity" that covers her deep despair from most of the people in her life is beginning to crumble here as I mirror back her rather well hidden truths.

This is where we connect emotionally. I am witnessing and describing the life she is bearing. As painful as this can be, there can be a sense of relief in being seen by another and not hurt or humiliated in the process.

We both have the courage required to begin this journey. We have stepped into the relationship, the vessel of her analysis.

CHAPTER 4

First Dreams and Drawings

The morning after our first extended meeting
   Laura returns to my office. We had planned this because of her long commute. A friend of hers living in a nearby town had welcomed her overnight visit. Entering the office Laura seems physically comfortable, with good eye contact, expressing no hesitation to begin our session. At the end of her initial phone call several weeks ago, I had encouraged her to remember a dream that might arise before our initial face-to-face session. Today we will have time to look at this together.
   Laura is not aware of the great significance of the initial dream, the one she has before our first session, although I am, as we enter this session. In the beginning of a Jungian analysis, the initial dream is seen as a *commentary* on the state of the individual's psychic organization. It is prognostic and it is a communication from her unconsciousness to me, her therapist. It is also information for her if she is able to pay attention. This initial dream describes her concerns and often indicates direction in the analytic work to come.
   Taking out her notebook, Laura reads the dream she had after our first phone conversation, before we met face to face. She also shows me small images that she sketched after writing the dream in her notebook. Laura reads these dreams aloud to me:

Dream: The Stones

4 a.m. Image: Six small stones lined up (tied together) on a cord.

6:30 a.m. Image: A monolith partially buried in sand or earth. Large, dark, heavy.

From Laura's notes: Floods of tears, crying, I can't bear to be disconnected. Want to stay connected forever. Wish to arrange the stones in a meaningful way – make some sense of what is happening. Upon waking, sensed only the rock without the landscape. Back to sleep until 9:30 a.m. when the landscape idea (not in the dream) came to me. Very unusual to sleep this long. All summer/fall been sleeping less and less 3, 4, or 5 hours until this week. Represents what is dark, hidden, too enormous to lift – but the top is uncovered, clearly visible. The work I have been doing on my own? The stones represent the arrangement of my hopes for relief to come from working with P. Crying as I write this.

She sits in silence looking down at the drawings after reading.

I listen as she reads the dream. I listen to the selection of her words, her vocabulary and sentence structure, and the dream images, symbols. I study her facial and bodily expression and notice how she is breathing. I watch her as she shares her carefully drawn, delicate pen sketches. These sketches are her attempts to illustrate her dream images for herself and for me. Drawing is a way of communicating *below words*. Laura indicates this notebook is specifically used as a dream journal where she makes small sketches and records her thoughts, reflections, and emotions. She brings so much of herself here so soon; for this I am very glad.

It is unusual for a patient to commence her work in such a well-prepared manner. I see she is in the habit of recording her inner life and expressing herself through art with no outside prompting or encouragement on my part.

I welcome her dream and drawings. I feel happy that she can share so much of herself. My trust in this process of healing relationships within a life is stirred. I hope that I can reflect the essence of my long training for her benefit. I know that healing is an ongoing life process; analysis or psychotherapy is not curing. Problems may be solved along the way. There is no cure for being a human being.

Laura hands me the page of pen-and ink-sketches. I hold the page of images on my lap as we prepare to reflect on the on these first dreams, actually a pair of dreams, that rise out of her unconscious. First there is an image of six small stones that are connected, held together, by a cord. The stone is indeed a profound symbol: the basic foundation, the mineral matter of earth. I see that a cord is connecting the six small stones. The second image drawn is dream two, a monolith, a rectangular shaped solid rock, rising out of the earth and sand. This single immense stone is partly exposed, partly hidden.

It appears that Laura's psyche has a language rich with ancient symbols.

Many people have trouble remembering dreams and, with patience, must learn a process of remembering and valuing these subtle messages from the unconscious mind. Few people initially report dreams with this elemental weight or gravity. Laura, who already practices recording her dreams in a journal, has just brought profound archetypal images: stones and a monolith, ancient symbols of the totality of the Self. Human life is brief and stone suggests eternity.

Stones represent the indestructible material of transformation. Laura has brought a dream uncovering stone. There is a solid core within and the mystery of life is starting to be revealed.

We sit quietly with the drawings for some time. It is important that she reflects upon the images, "feeling them", sensing them in her body and accessing memory. Emotions and feelings need space for expression. Sometimes it is too difficult to put this into words. Her wealth of thoughts and feelings may not surface initially. Most of us have to learn to focus our attention inward to remember dream images and notice bodily feelings. We need to find a way to express and describe our internal experiences that are generally invisible to others. This requires a felt sense of safety in the presence of another person. I am aware that my relationship with Laura is in a beginning stage.

While waiting for Laura to return to words and make comments, I am seeing in my mind and reflecting thoughts to myself, not spoken aloud to Laura. I see collected and organized stones on a cord and second, the partly revealed monolith: an enormous, rectangular-shaped stone. The two images appear to be static and solid although perhaps hewn or shaped by human hands. The composition of stone is mineral composed of highly organized crystalline forms visible in their complexity only with microscopes and other magnifying equipment. Seeing the structure of stone is well below our normal level of awareness. Stones are ancient prehistoric records of the beginning of time of the earth. Discovered in many places, the monolith, an exceptionally large standing stone, was erected by early humans and generally associated with spiritual and religious meaning.

Laura begins her analysis by bringing dreams echoing the history of the planet's core elements from the universe, the cosmos, and she also brings her personal history to these images. With these dreams I feel the rich potential ahead if Laura is able to access and make use the vastness offered to her by her unconscious.

Laura begins to describe stones and then the monolith in a landscape. Both are in a context without people or other obvious life. She says, "The first image of six smaller stones on a cord shows some form of organizing by someone." She continues, "The cord is some kind of material, maybe woven threads or skin, sinew? It's stringing the six small stones together. I'm not sure what this is, what it's for." Being an artist appears to allow Laura access to visual imagery, a gift.

I am thinking to myself that this image signals that there is an unseen organizing capacity in the unconsciousness. The cord or thread has the function of relating and connecting six smaller stones. I choose not to share my reflections now. From past experience, if I do, I am likely to interfere with her responses by directing or by inhibiting her own inner work. It is important that Laura does not depend on me to tell her the meanings. She has to find her personal meaning. There may be an appropriate time in the future for me to share my thoughts and amplify the meaning of these symbols gathered from many cultures over time.

She reads her reflections from her dream journal:

The stones represent hopes for my relief to come from this work.

"Belonging to a group is essential to me." Laura says. She then describes her passionate wish to belong, to be connected to others. While I am observing her, she shifts her voice tone from passionate expression to a quiet appraisal and reflection.

Inwardly I am thinking that stones on a cord were used as primitive counting devices. If such a cord is tied end to end, it may be used as a necklace, a rosary or *mala, meditation* beads. Sacred internal utterances or prayers are made as the user touches the stones. I am reminded of linear time, division and sequencing of hours, days and months, I also think about the passage of time as an eternal circle. Stones on a cord indicate division. Could this be the division of time? The whole or eternal present is divided and then marked by the stones, like knots.

Laura begins describing her personal associations, quite different from my thoughts, about the stones, "I am reading a book of essays by Susan Griffin, *A Chorus of Stones: The Private Life of War*.[6] She is writing on the meaning of war. I'd like to read a small piece to you." She reaches into her bag and takes out a well-worn paperback book and turns to a dog-eared page. She reads, "… all history, including the history of each family, is a part of us, such that, when we hear any secret revealed, a secret about a grandfather, or an uncle, or a secret about the battle of Dresden in 1945, our lives are made suddenly clearer to us, as the unnatural heaviness of unspoken truth is dispersed. For perhaps we are like stones; our own history and the history of the world embedded in us, we hold a sorrow deep within and cannot weep until that history is sung."

She stops reading from the book, places it on the couch next to where she is sitting and looks at me directly. Speaking quietly, she tells me her hope for "relief."

She waited a long time to begin this exploration of her own inner life with the help of a Jungian therapist, a trained analyst. She tells me that she had some psychotherapy years ago in the wake of marital and family issues. The doctor was a warm and helpful man; she felt it was a positive experience. She has worked with her own thoughts and feelings internally and has read widely for many years. She had begun to discuss the ideas of Carl Jung with her relative in California who is a psychotherapist and found that helpful. Laura relates that she was deeply impressed and began to read and inform herself about the psychology of the unconscious.

She stops and then says: "At this same time, out of the blue, I received the phone call from Alex." She begins to describe to me her experience of this unexpected transatlantic call. The call was unexpected, shocking; it served to open a well or a tomb of feelings. In her vulnerable state Laura felt compelled to take the risk of opening herself in therapy. "It was at this time I realized that I needed outside help. I called you," she says.

I am aware that Laura has returned to her description of why she decided to enter into an analysis: "a broken heart." She is revealing her deepest emotional longing. We are beginning the work of weaving her personal history with unresolved losses and needs, building a trusting therapeutic relationship together, and moving into working with her dream material, her relationship with the unconscious. The image of the cord of stones acted as a bridge to her memories of WWII, Alex, loss of innocence, family deaths and losses.

We move on to the second dream, which contains the image of a dark, heavy monolith, which is partly buried in earth and partly exposed. I am looking at her sketch. Laura expresses that the monolith in her dream is "awesome and evokes feelings of mystery. Now, in relation to this specific image, she talks about the 1968 film *2001: A Space Odyssey*.[7] One of the important opening scenes includes a monolith. She felt the image was awesome, an intersection of human evolution, the history of war, religion, art, and science.

She reflects on her husband Eugene, "In the 1960s he was a scientist working in optics. He'd immerse himself for days and nights, working for NASA. "Much of that time he was away working with telescopes. For a time he practically lived in Hawaii," says Laura. "I held the family together and worked part time. I really missed him. I felt so lonely."

"The image of a very large smooth black rectangular monolith is used near the beginning of the film. The setting was a vast plain in prehistoric time. The ape-like creatures were depicted at what seemed the dawning of consciousness and the discovery of tool making for hunting, for brute superiority, and for survival. The ape-like creatures encounter a large black monolith, partly buried in the earth. At first they are terrified then they ambivalently approach it, showing awe.

They were also curious" Laura says. I am now more aware of the great importance of the monolith in Laura's dream image.

I remember, not speaking of this to Laura, that I too saw the film in 1968 and was very moved. I was living in Washington, D.C. and saw it in a small art theater: "The Janus," the name for the image of dual masks of tragedy and comedy in ancient Greece: the human condition.

"The story is about a space journey with danger, secrets, conflict, murder, advanced machines and mystery, and maybe reincarnation," Laura says. I hear urgency in her voice and listen deeply as she remembers details of the story aloud. "The main character is an astronaut facing a crisis on a spaceship that is on an important mission to seek intelligent life associated with the discovery of a black monolith on the moon. Onboard the spaceship the astronauts begin to sense that the highly advanced computer they name "H. A. L." (*Heuristically programmed algorithmic computer*) has its own, divergent, plans. H. A. L. takes control of the spaceship and shuts off the life support for the astronauts and scientists onboard. The last astronaut surviving, the story's hero, is finally able to disarm H.A.L.'s higher artificial intelligence programs, as one might perform a lobotomy on a human. The astronaut escapes immediate death. He travels alone in a small spacecraft, drifting toward Jupiter. The vessel becomes caught in the planet's gravitational fields and travels at warp-speed, outside of the experience of time, as we know it. This is depicted through dramatic visual effects. Inexplicably, the astronaut finds himself in a strange, very formal room with echoing sounds. He recognizes himself in a mirror and now finds that he is a very old man. Instantly he is sitting alone eating, next he's in a bed rapidly aging, and then dying. An enigmatic fetus simultaneously appears in an orb floating in space with the earth below suggesting that new life begins."

I know that the film uses powerful archetypal symbols and themes: monolith, journey, cooperation and conflict, war, outer space/cosmos/galaxy/universe/infinity, death, and rebirth. As I listen to Laura telling the story, I hear that the story, symbols, and the time of the 1960s are profoundly meaningful to her. This story links many levels of personal and collective meaning simultaneously.

Her initial dream is giving me a significant glimpse into themes of deep importance in her life; she is not fully aware of the significance now. She begins to share her own associations to the mythic symbols of the film and her dreams: "The monolith in the film seems to be describing something mysterious, awesome, something possibly placed there by more intelligent life," Laura says, "The ape-like creatures are afraid at first, then are drawn together to reach toward or touch it.

Maybe it's about our beginnings as humans. Maybe we are always drawn toward something we can't understand." Laura's dreams of the stones on a cord and a monolith have an ancient quality. We look at her drawings together; I feel and its hard to put this in words, the presence of mystery as we contemplate this cosmic, mythic story, her dreams, and associations. She is remembering this period of her personal life, creative work, marriage and family. She is beginning to gather and narrate her history, her own life story. She is telling me about her life through her memories, stories, dreams, images, and associations.

Being early in this treatment, we are barely beginning to construct a safe "container" or trusting relationship. It is not the time to amplify the symbols, which would be quite interesting although distracting now. It is the time to be present with her experience, to listen to her language, tone of voice, her descriptions of her history and the landscape of her inner world. I pay attention to my feelings; I am moved.

Every person has her own inner geography of voices and images, themes, stories, and characters. Archetypes are hypothetical, theoretical constructs of universal concepts and themes such as story, father, mother, teacher, journey, marriage, war, and love in the unconscious, naming only a few. We each have our own way of seeing and clothing, or dressing, the universal forms of myths, and stories within our specific culture, historical epoch, and collective psyche.

My mind, my psyche, is stimulated by her drawings and description of the film's archetypal themes: beginnings and endings, evolution, life and death, universal mystery, time, past, present and future and "the journey". The themes in her story evoke the ancient circular symbol of the *uroboros*[8], often depicted as a Serpent whose body forms a circle as he bites his own tail, is it self-devouring, eternal, or both? It is a symbol of self-containment of all beginnings and endings, the carrier of *all* within itself. Laura's dream and her associations to a personal and culturally important film remind me of the circular, self-contained process we all experience universally: birth and death, confronting conflict and mystery in the journey of life, relationships with others, and our aloneness: our individuation process.

Alchemy, as used in Jung's psychology[9] based on a medieval form of chemistry, is a symbolic process describing psychological transformation and maturation in an individual. The work of holding the tension of the seemingly opposite experiences, the physical material world– including our body– and the spiritual experience is necessary for transformation. Jung's theories describe the work of psychological transformation of unconscious patterns by raising them to consciousness through working with dreams, imagination, discussion and memory. Individuation is the personal expression and journey of a life. Analysis can become an analogue or parallel process to the symbolic, medieval art of alchemy, the object of which is transformation of the *lead* of unconsciousness, into, or toward the *gold* of illuminated consciousness. As described in ancient alchemy, the *nigredo* is the beginning of the process. It connotes darkness that is barely penetrable, chaos. One's mind is dense and can be dull, without illumination or understanding, and one's mood is experienced as heavy, depressed. Psychologically, depression is a symptomatic experience associated with this heavy darkness. I feel that Laura's dream monolith– dark and heavy – describes the beginning of her alchemical process. The unconscious with its darkness and chaos is the beginning of individuation. In other words, this is the process of her coming to consciousness, to know, accept and, possibly transform, and be transformed in and through dreams and life's journey.

In Laura's dream the image the monolith is partly revealed and partly hidden. The source of all images is buried deep within the unconscious. I note that there are no humans or mammals present in her initial dream. It presents the mystery of life on earth and possibly beyond. The cord could be used as a tool. I wonder to myself if we are glimpsing the ancient idea of the mythic philosopher's stone. Symbolically, the philosopher's stone is a substance that the medieval alchemists believed could be used to convert lead into gold.

Listening as Laura touches upon the images and their meaning to her, I ask, "Why now, why do these images appear now?"

Laura takes her time to answer. "I don't know. The place in the dream feels ancient. I suppose that is why I have come here, to unearth myself." Laura weeps for what seems a very long time as we sit without talking. My intuition is that this dream landscape is also a description of her profound and deep loneliness as a human being.

She is feeling stored sadness from so many experiences in her history. It is easier to remember and discuss the high times and the excitement of her creative career. Now the fatigue from her life's heaviness: her work, the pain of losses, and her current depression are very much in her consciousness. The images put forth by her psyche describe her interior experience.

In tears, Laura says: "I cry when I read the dreams out loud to you. Why?" Pondering this for a moment, I answer: "When you read dreams to me you have an invested witness, person. You do not need to take care of me. Perhaps this allows you the space for your own feelings."

Gathering her sweater and small cloth bag for her notebook, pen, the book she was reading, and her car keys, she gets up and slowly walks toward the door. "I'll be staying tonight in Arlington, she says. "My friend Elizabeth offered me a spare room and doesn't require that I visit with her when I get in late. I'll have time alone for reflection and reading."

Looking at me tenderly, she sighs and adds, "Thank you for being here." I feel the weight of her depression and the intensity of her suffering, and I wonder what lies ahead.

CHAPTER 5

Nakedness, the Dog, Art, and Reflection

We meet the following week.

Laura is cheerful as she arrives. She slept little last night, as usual. "I really don't need much sleep. I'm glad to begin this work," she tells me. She brought her dream from last night, carefully recorded in her notebook. I listen as she reads:

Dream: after beginning with P.

> *I look down and see I am naked. I move to the foot of the bed where I can see into another room. A dog is there, very happy, wagging its tail and looking at what seems an opening in the wall, which turns out to be a painting, semi-abstract, propped up against the far corner of the room. There is a glass covering the painting in which I can begin to see my reflection. The dog continues to wag its tail. He's very happy, with an erection. Gradually the two images of the dog and of me begin to merge. I awake thinking of the symbolism of this merger, feeling tremendously empowered, particularly about painting, but also about proceeding with my life without deliberate reliance on the men in my life.*

She looks up from her notes. "I'm trying to find a way to see my own possibilities and do this on my terms. I've been relying on the men in my life for my self-worth." She pauses, "The dog's joy—I want that too." She smiles. "The painting is under glass. I love that there's a painting in my dream."

I listen to Laura's dream and see her attention and curiosity. She leans forward, her voice tone is somewhat lifted from last week's deep depression. I am seeing that Laura immediately begins to respond positively to our work together. We are building the foundation of a relationship, and we are playing with the images together. She appears to be able to receive my reflections from the two previous sessions of her life's struggles and issues. I am sensing that she is feeling welcome and safe enough to continue coming to see me after such personal revelations and expression of feelings that rose so quickly when we met earlier. Her risk of becoming vulnerable in my presence is a positive experience for her. I show a sincere interest in both her outer and inner life. She reports feeling somewhat relieved and is clearly making an initial attachment to me and to the analytic work.

I am aware that her unconscious responds quickly and immediately with a dream that she is able to record. I see that she is in the habit of writing. She takes notes carefully, partly from the practice of years of participating in professional meetings.

In the dream I see that there is a symbolic merger, a composite overlay of the dog, the painting, and Laura's reflection in the glass at the completion of the dream. She is also aware of it. Her psyche is bringing aspects of herself together into one complex, layered image.

Laura's dream portrays her naked: *I look down and see I am naked.* Here she has no persona, no social mask, no role, or rank. She is simply a human being with the support of a bed inside a room. This is *her* first dream as a character or actor within the dream. She is appearing naked, without defenses, either physical or psychological. Remarkably, in the dream she is not exhibiting shame; she is not demonstrating the impulse to cover herself or flee.

We all have some feeling of nakedness in the presence of a trained therapist, doctor, or psychologist, especially in early sessions. We have an expectation that we are transparent although this is not true. Yet in the beginning of a psychological treatment most of us do not dream of our nakedness so immediately, and if we do, we may not share it with a therapist we hardly know. Laura appears ready to reveal herself. Her emotional pain is revealing itself in our sessions, and she is consciously, willingly, seeking help. I feel that Laura is resonating deeply with me in some place, some state, *below words,* in her being. Certainly this is happening in me. I think she feels seen by me. Safety is developing.

We begin talking about the dream beginning with the image of her nakedness. She is looking down, seeing her body, realizing something about herself at this moment. She describes feeling comfortable, not self-conscious or inhibited. Laura finds the word she wants, "unconstrained". We do not talk about the deeper meanings of the bed as a place and vehicle of transformation: rest, sleep, dreaming, love, affection, sexuality, birth, illness, and death. Today she is more comfortable just reporting this dream, not moving further into a bodily felt experience.

As Laura and I continue our discussion, she is aware that *she* appears as herself in the dream. She is both an observing presence and the main character in this dream space. "I would say your ego is the observer of the room, the animal, the wall, and the painting," I say. We both express to each other that she is moving *toward* the foot of the bed, possibly motivated by curiosity and interest. She is clearly not moving away from anyone or thing. She says she is not motivated by a state of fear but by a state of attraction. In the dream Laura is quite awake and actively engaging. She sees the dog who is *"very happy, wagging its tail and looking into an opening in the wall."* She is seeing that beyond the bed, an animal instinct is present, not a dangerous instinct but a friendly companion animal. The dog is focused on and interested in what seems to be an opening in the wall. I say that the dog, which I would normally expect to be more emotionally connected or related to a nearby human, seems to be seeing, smelling, and sensing something else very interesting to him, perhaps in the opening in the wall or beyond. The dog appears in a state of pleasurable anticipation, including having an erection. There appears to be an opening in a wall, yet on closer examination within the dream, Laura is seeing that this is actually a painting, a created image on a two-dimensional surface. Laura and I agree that things are not always what they appear to be. This is a rather magical aspect of the dream. This painting is a creative semiabstract work of art and is covered with glass, which is serving as a protective covering. Here the glass also becomes reflective, acting as a mirror. It becomes a *looking glass*. She is seeing herself in the glass reflection and also seeing the dog's reflection. Laura's reflection, the dog's reflection, and the semiabstract painting become a single complex reflection.

"The dog, with his erection, has a joyful sense and lots of energy," Laura says. "I wake up thinking of the symbolism of this merger and feel tremendously empowered, particularly about painting."

As I listen to her speaking I think about what an unusual expression of creativity this dream presents, so multilayered and discriminating. This dream is indicating that Laura will find herself in reflection, in her instincts, and in creative artwork. All of these can be understood as a door in a wall, two-dimensional and concrete, but instead it becomes another kind of opening into a painting, into the realm of imagination. Her instinctual being is a vibrant male dog.

The appearance of a companion animal in a dream at the beginning of a treatment is a relief to me. I am not facing primitive beasts at the start of treatment, such as a mythic dragon or wild animals such as a lion. This dog is not a wild and uncontained animal energy that could overwhelm Laura's ego or the analysis before we establish a strong attachment.

Artists are especially capable of experiencing loss of ego boundaries, even time, in the midst of their concentration and fascination with the subject or medium. Artists have the capacity to open themselves to images, colors, sounds, smells, textures, patterns, and feelings of others. We can benefit, be enriched, when artists share and express their discoveries with us. Life can feel more meaningful when we open to the arts and music, especially to what is perceived as beautiful.

Laura reminisces, "We had such a wonderful male Labrador retriever at that time when the children were almost adolescents. We were living in California. It was such a busy and engaged time of life. We were outside a lot in the beautiful weather and constantly in motion. The dog frequently jumped the fence and we'd go chasing him around the neighborhood. He loved the game, the chase."

This family dog represents grounded everyday life, a normalized life that Laura identifies with in her second marriage. This family dog carries memories of joyful, raucous and playful relationships with family. These experiences were reparative and healing. In her first marriage, her mother-in-law and husband gave the family dog away. It was a wrenching loss during the time she was hospitalized for breast cancer. Her attempt to have a healthy nuclear family in her first marriage failed. This dream dog has an erection, an embodied healthy libido. The dog's erection signals potential fertility and new life.

In bringing this dream into the session I learn that Laura can dream about and openly discuss sexuality. Her dream indicates that she has an assertive, phallic, masculine energy within. This masculine dog is associated with her creative possibilities and pleasure. She associates this dog with her Labrador retriever. This breed goes after things and brings them home. I would say this dream dog is in service to her ego; he is possibly an inner helper or guide.

I feel that this dream indicates that her unconscious psyche has engaged, in a lively way, both Laura and me. The painting's content as a form of creative expression is semi abstract. What does this mean? What is the nature of abstract art? It will take time to find the patterns, organization, and meaning in Laura's psychological work. *Semi* abstract might mean we can find some familiar images in the picture: Laura and a dog, and other new forms and themes that may emerge if she allows herself to imagine what this new painting is bringing to consciousness.

In Laura's initial associations, I am hearing her wish to become more self-reliant and to become differentiated from the men she had depended upon in the past for her power and self-worth. I see that her psyche can respond quickly through a dream to our initial sessions and engage with a wonderful, even humorous, complexity. The dream has a lively, hopeful feeling for both of us.

The experience of remembering, recording, and then reading a dream aloud to another who is interested is a powerful act and often experienced by the dreamer as healing. Deeper meaning can be found and integrated in a slower, reflective, analytic experience. When Laura associates and explores the images for meaning and experiences and feels her words and story, it is like opening a sealed letter or a book. Engagement and relationship with the unconscious has an organic quality. We will never find all the meanings of dreams; the unconscious is vast, like the ocean, the cosmos. I listen and have intuitions of meaning that I hold, waiting for Laura to find her own meanings at her own pace. As she becomes more confident and secure associating to her dreams and remembering parts of her life I will join her more with my own reflections and intuitions.

CHAPTER 6

Nuclear Family History

Laura's analysis continues steadily, twice weekly for extended sessions through the autumn into winter. If she lived closer to Boston our meetings would be spread out over the week in shorter sessions. Most people come once a week for Jungian analysis, some twice. Laura has ego strength, time, capacity, and motivation to enter into this process at an accelerated rate.

Laura is comfortable driving, enjoys it. Her long drive from Vermont south to the Boston area travels through stretches of rolling hills, across farmland, by forests, and near small towns. The richness and natural beauty of the seasons becomes a part of the ritual of treatment. She drives by the modest, old, Green Mountains, evergreens, and open space. As the time passes the road winds into and through autumn's radiant colors eventually followed by the whiteness of winter snowstorms. Grey sky eventually becomes blue. The melting snow reveals the soft green growth of early spring.

She continues to use her friend's spare room throughout her treatment. Reading and writing into the nights, Laura dives deep into our process, immersing her mind, body, and heart.

She talks about her first experience with psychotherapy in the 1950s, when she was about twenty-six years old. That was the time of her initial cancer diagnosis and treatment, illness, and infections of hepatitis B and C. This was also the time of her decision to divorce her first husband. She engaged in several years of psychotherapy with a male psychiatrist, an experience she described as "good." She felt that her doctor had offered her fatherly concern and advice. "He was a good father figure and I needed this," she says. "He listened deeply to me, something I didn't have in my father who was absent so much of the time. I didn't have this with my first husband, who was frequently unavailable to me emotionally. Dr. Karl was someone I felt I could trust."

Over many months Laura records dreams upon waking, sometimes making sketches. She always brings her dream journal into our analytic sessions. Laura interweaves details of her history throughout sessions over time, along with her current daily life concerns, and future plans. In any one session we touch on the past, the present, and sometimes the future. We continue working well together.

While in analysis, in and outside of our face-to-face meetings, she is slowly remembering and experiencing much that has been held in her unconscious, dreams often help. They allow small portions of pain and psychological difficulty to be revealed. This process of slow change, drop by drop over time, allows our conscious mind time to metabolize and integrate the experiences into the context of our conscious life.

Laura's more easily accessible conscious concerns relate to her current marriage and family, and her older child, her daughter, Karen. Her life and care have been an ongoing challenge.

When Karen was about sixteen she began acting in disturbing and self-defeating ways following a car accident. She had been driving and suffered head trauma, a concussion that required stitches. Laura didn't remember if CT scans were performed as part of the medical protocol in the 1960s. Not long after the injury, Karen began to have numerous difficulties high school. She attempted and failed to hold a series of part-time jobs. Enormously discouraged at the state of her life and depressed, Karen at age seventeen attempted suicide with wrist cutting and an overdose of pills at home. Karen was hospitalized for several months. Her younger brother Mark was at home when this occurred.

"Mark was losing his older sister to an head injury or a frightening mental illness, or both," Laura said, covering her face with her hands. "He witnessed helplessly as his sister was carried from our home and committed to a hospital."

This was a profoundly distressing, family-shattering experience. The loss of stability, safety, order, and emotional connection is traumatic for any family. Frightening and tragic events like severe injury and attempted suicide cause every family member to suffer and be thrown into confusion, shame, anxiety, sadness, and sometimes anger. Disrupted daily routines and life plans inevitably cause feelings of helplessness. Each member feels some failure for failing to prevent the tragedy.

I wait for Laura to compose herself. "It was a terrible nightmare," she says slowly, "emergency hospital attendants forcefully taking Karen, who physically was struggling, away from home. Eugene was there; we were all confused. We didn't know the right thing to do. It was horrible."

After her hospitalization, Karen tried again to live at home and attend school. Her efforts continually fell apart. Laura and Eugene tried different schools. The outpatient psychiatric help they found for her wasn't enough. "Karen told me that everything was betraying her and that life was impossible," Laura says. "She withdrew into her room. Socializing was too painful. None of us could really imagine the hell she was in. Later, after numerous treatments in several residential facilities, it was clear that she was descending into a psychosis. Medications only subdued some symptoms, but nothing really helped her." Laura inhales sharply, looks away, crying, closing her eyes tightly, and brings her arms up over her chest, over her heart. She is in deep emotional pain. Finally she takes a breath.

Laura turns back to look at me pointedly. "Was it an underlying brain problem?" she asks. "Was it schizophrenia? Was it the head injury in the car accident? Was it the medication I was given when I was pregnant with her? Was it genetic? Was I a failure as a mother? " Laura couldn't protect Mark from this terrible unraveling of his older sister's life. I have no doubt that this series of traumatic events was deeply wounding for her son Mark. Laura's love of her children and investment in their lives is evident, as is her confusion, shame, and sense of failure.

The tragedy of mental illness is difficult for all family members, weighing especially heavily on Laura, on any mother.

She reported that Karen and Mark's biological father was unable to participate in Karen's treatment and did not financially help with the overwhelming expenses. His communication was not dependable and his visits were inconsistent. His lack of consistency was extremely disappointing for Laura. She initiated meetings with her primary physician and Dr. Karl, her former psychiatrist. He met with Karen. He interviewed and evaluated her. Consulting with other colleagues, the physicians concurred and recommended that the best course of treatment was to support continuing psychiatric hospitalization with the possibly of long-term residential care. Living at home was impossible and heart breaking.

Karen spent months in a private psychiatric hospital; it was not a realistic long-term solution for her care. Laura tells me that she continues to seek better treatments for her daughter and follows research on schizophrenia. Currently Karen is in a halfway home and attends a psychiatric day program. Laura is exploring the most humane and helpful facilities in the country. Her ex-husband remains in her children's lives in a very limited way. "Nick is very important to Mark. He talks about his visits with his father. I think it's important for Karen too although..." her words trail off.

I reflect to myself that the younger son lost his older sister as playmate and his adolescent friend. They were "pals, good buddies," Laura said, "until the accident when Karen was sixteen." As I have not met with Mark or the family; I do not know what feelings or realities are true for them. It is not difficult to imagine that Mark could feel irrationally responsible, or even experience survivor's guilt, wondering why he was spared illness. Mark was unable to save or rescue his older sister. The siblings of ill or mentally disturbed sisters and brothers may feel helpless, and, they are often unintentionally emotionally neglected in the crises, chaos and aftermath. Parents lose the child they knew and imagined into the future. They struggle to accept the unfathomable child now present or hospitalized. This *stranger* is confusing, sometimes frightening, and unable to communicate with clarity. Siblings, relatives, friends, and community are unsure how to relate or help.

Laura's life energy, and a good deal of the family's finances were, and continue to be, devoted to the details of a support system for Karen. This comes at the expense of other family members and herself. Laura visits, writes, and dreams of her. Karen is now unable to live in New England with the family where she had endangered herself by wandering away from home without cost, hat, or boots in the bitter cold New England winter. On visits at home she acted inappropriately, although not aggressively, toward others and behaved dangerously: failing to turn off stove burners, carelessly leaving burning cigarettes around, and other minor disturbing behaviors. The family was advised to have Karen hospitalized in a more temperate climate with the possibility of a halfway home to follow. This is the advice they are following now.

These family difficulties are compounded by the realities of a blended family system: four stepchildren, two from each partner. Each child has specific emotional needs, physical needs, and a unique history. Eugene's children had their own challenges with that disruptive divorce which their mother fought in court battles. In addition Eugene's children had their own traumatic experiences in earlier years.

Children of divorce can be additionally hindered in emotional development by confusing communication, parental tension, and the child's irrational guilt, neglect, along with many other issues. Competition over parents' limited amount of time for practical attention and emotional investment, as well as competition over social and financial resources, are inevitable and appear to be true in this family.

The greatest obvious challenge to Laura and her family is Karen's deterioration into chronic mental illness, leading to emotional and physical separation from them. "This was and continues to be a strange kind of living hell with no resolution, no completion," she says. "These are losses with no end in sight. Karen's illness is severe and chronic."

Following these family disruptions, younger son Mark struggled to construct a future. He wondered about higher education. He thought about and tried several careers. It wasn't easy for him to move forward. Always interested in writing; he followed the growing edge of technology and media and decided to pursue this. "He is often away and has become increasingly inaccessible," Laura says, "He's unavailable, especially emotionally in these past few years. He returned to the States after several years in Munich, Germany. He doesn't reveal much of that part of his life to me." She continues to see him when she accompanies Eugene on business travel to Stanford University. Mark keeps a small apartment south of San Francisco. She makes herself available to him and is open to anything he wants to discuss.

From the view of psychological development, I can see that Laura's younger son felt compelled to leave home and to establish his own identity in the face of Laura and Eugene's work successes and his sister's illness. Like all young adults Mark must find his own way in life. Laura talks of missing him and feeling guilty that she was not available enough in his early childhood while working as a single mother. She then fell in love with Eugene, and during her children's adolescence, she was immersed in helping him with research projects. Once Karen's crises began to unfold Laura's attention was increasingly preoccupied with her daughter's problems in daily life.

Laura expresses worry about what will happen when Mark is older. I am wondering if she is also thinking about her own future. She clearly wants a more mature relationship with Mark now as an adult, and struggles to reach him as well as worrying about her daughter's complex future.

Most children are angry, some quite justifiably, toward parents in a divorce. Withdrawal can also be a form of passive anger. As I am Laura's therapist, not her family's, I am not aware of Mark's actual relationship with his biological father, his experience of his older sister, his thoughts and feelings about Laura, Eugene, or the course and content of his life. I can only work with Laura's report. I will never know how accurate or self-deceptive a report is and must rely on intuition and experience.

As our sessions together progress, I can see that Laura is striving to come to terms with her failures, real and imagined, as a mother. She is realizing that she cannot undo the past but she can work to find personal meaning in her suffering. She must grieve and mourn her losses and accept her human failings. Can she forgive herself? Laura can make the effort and take responsibility to act differently in her relationships as she moves forward in her life.

We return to her dreams to explore all the possible meanings that her initial dream could possibly have for her. Layers of the meaning of dreams unfold over time. For example, the stones held together on a cord could be related to the binding together of the blended family. Each of the six stones could represent a member of her family. The connection is there; they are clearly bound together with a rough cord. The second image, the enigmatic monolith, could also represent the mystery of her daughter's psychosis: awesome, dark, impenetrable, and of enormous weight. Laura accepts the possibility of these personal and symbolic meanings.

CHAPTER 7

The Eagle Dream

In our session today Laura says that before her initial call to me many months ago, she flew across the country to one of Eugene's on-location projects. While visiting him in Los Alamos, New Mexico, she found that he was, once again, overextended and preoccupied. Emotional connection of any depth with him during these times did not seem possible. Laura spent time horseback riding in the high desert. Reviewing her frustrations, she reported feeling growing resentment, restlessness, and urgency.

She shares the important experience that she had in the desert and the powerful dream that followed. Reminiscent of an early pattern of behavior in her youth, she retreated to the outdoors and found comfort in nature. There under a vast sky and open land she reviewed her life. In the desert she began to realize the depth of her sorrow, the disappointments in her marriages and in her life. Laura felt the intensity of her loneliness and the pain and sorrow of so many losses. During one of the nights following a day of solo time horseback riding in the wilderness, Laura recorded a significant dream of conflict between an eagle and a falcon. Her dream allows her a glimpse into her violent inner struggle.

Dream: In the desert. I am in a field facing west, in the West with others. The land is flat and I can see for miles except for places behind brush–sagebrush, tumbleweed, and mesquite. There are small groups of people scattered here and there. Suddenly I see an eagle with its wings completely outspread, falling straight to earth, surely to its death. There is blood on it, lots of it. It strikes the ground headfirst as it holds its wings rigidly away from its body. Everyone gasps both at the beauty of the creature, its size and perfection and the sight of its impending doom. But as soon as the bird hits the ground it soars back into the sky again, high up, rapidly, and we all see that a smaller bird, a hawk or falcon, is following it from the exact spot where the eagle struck. The smaller bird is also bloodied and the two do a ballet like this, repeating their rising and falling, following one another in turns. This is repeated two or three

*times. Each time the birds fall to earth, they are behind some vegetation
and cannot be seen. The final time we see the eagle rise into the sky it is
no longer followed by the falcon. There is a feeling of utter triumph, of
freedom, and I realize that I am the eagle.*

In horseback riding, she found self-comfort in nature, an effective
way of soothing and containing herself, her feelings. She realized how
deeply alone she'd felt for so many years. Lifelong needs and wishes
had begun to overwhelm her. Her unresolved past experiences were
reactivating and coming to consciousness. In analytic terms, "the return of the repressed" memories and feelings. After over fifty years of
demanding trials with health, family, and work in the world, Laura's
psychological defenses were now fragile, permeable; their former was
effectiveness failing. For the first time in her adult life she unconsciously created the time and space to face herself.

Months after she begins her analysis with me, she brings the Eagle
dream into her session.

Laura says: "This dream was powerfully moving and inspiring. I
did not understand it then although I knew this dream showed me that
a profound life and death struggle was happening in me. I knew I was
witnessing something spiritual."

Laura and I reflect on the setting of the dream: *In the desert. I am
in a field, facing west.* Entering the desert has long been associated
with retreat to an isolated place for the purpose of spiritual revelation.
A field is an open, undefined, natural place. Facing west in symboli-
cal terms is facing introversion, incubation, hibernation, possibly death
and renewal. The sun sets in the west; the light disappears. "The West"
is a place, both real and imagined, in the American psyche that describes the pioneering spirit, a sense of open spaces, and the potential
of a new way of life. From her personal family history Laura reflects:
"The possibilities of The West drew my grandmother to New Mexico
during the Great Depression. She found her way to her creative spirit
by becoming a painter. I too was drawn west to California, maybe I
was following in her footsteps." She speaks of horseback riding into
the high desert as, "Being at one with nature." Unconsciously profound
change was already underway.

In the dream setting the desert habitat includes native plants–
organic life that can exist, even thrive, without much water. They
appear to be surviving in a harsh environment, and perhaps, illustrate
Laura's emotional and spiritual life. *Going into the desert* is tradition-
ally and biblically a time of endurance, banishment, contemplation,
psychological introversion, and confrontation with one's demons and
temptations. In her dream, small anonymous groups of people are

"witnessing" presences. I feel these are aspects of Laura's observing ego, conscious parts of herself watching her life's process. The initial glimpse of the eagle is shocking to her and awesome to the witnesses. It appears *suddenly*. Through various accounts in stories and myth, glimpsing the Divine is just that: shocking, dramatic, dangerous, and often experienced as violent. The ego is eclipsed without its permission; the Self in its powerful numinosity takes over. The eagle is acting in a deadly way. It is terribly wounded and falling without obstruction. I wonder aloud, "How could any living thing survive this situation?" I note that the color red has appeared in the dream as blood, *there is blood on it*, the eagle and the falcon are *bloodied*. There is wounding, flesh torn, and blood is flowing out of bodies. In alchemy, the color red signifies *rubedo*, the passion and culmination of an embodied, incarnate life. The birds in this dream are raptors, powerfully aggressive and predatory. The spirit is wounded; the great bird of divine majesty is falling to earth. In mythology the hawk is associated with the capacity to communicate with the beyond. Also in her personal memory: Laura bled in her late miscarriage and Karen cut her wrists.

Is Laura's spirit in conflict? Is it in a dance? *The two (birds) do a ballet like this ... two to three repetitions*. Things appearing in twos or pairs can symbolize coming to consciousness; the opposites are present in a twosome, such as darkness and light. Relationship inevitably has tension. If Laura can hold and experience the tension, feeling the opposites, what will the third, the resolution? Something will be born out of the tension of the opposites. What is coming to consciousness in Laura? After the fall, the birds *cannot be seen behind some vegetation*. This is a mystery. In the dream we are not allowed to see what happens or how it happens: death, healing, reconstitution. The process is invisible, yet we see the outcome, resolution, climax. I feel that this is a dramatic, dynamic image of the interrelationship, or dance, of life and death. Laura wrote: *There is a feeling of utter triumph, of freedom, and I realize that I am the eagle*.

This dream is an epiphany, a sudden intuitive realization or a manifestation of divinity within. As she reads and discusses it here with me now Laura does not behave or appear to be conscious of, or directly in touch with, these profound feelings. She speaks about the dream but does not behave or appear physically involved in it. I do not sense her mood lifting or anything indicating an expansive, triumphant experience. I am not feeling that Laura senses freedom now. She does not seem to be emotionally or physically feeling the danger, the horror, or the ecstasy of the dream.

Though "reporting" the dream now, Laura had this dream many months ago. It is not really alive in her at this present moment; she is not open to the depth of emotional experience indicated.

I hope that we will return to this dream in the future when she is more emotionally available. It is too rich a dream to simply "report".

CHAPTER 8

The Unrequited Love Affair

"I think about seeing him," she says. Laura and Alex had periodically corresponded in the past about their parallel lives. He is married with children of his own in Germany, she tells me that hadn't heard his voice in years. His brief telephone message stirred her memories and feelings, which continue to flood and distress her. She feels heartache and conflict about the possibility of seeing him. The pressure of this suffering provided energy for her decision to begin analysis. She had felt lonely in her marriage these past ten years, her husband's work always in the foreground, and her adult children essentially emotionally inaccessible. She misses emotional connections; her small extended family and close friends are busy with their own needs and lives. Many live far away.

I feel it is time, after months of our work together, to look more closely at her relationship with Alex. I want to learn more about him and ask her questions. "Alex and I carried on phone conversations for nearly a month after his initial call," Laura says.

I'm realizing that Laura chose not to speak of their ongoing telephone relationship in our early months of analysis. I'm surprised that she didn't feel safe enough, trusting enough, to talk about the ongoing calls until now. I under estimated her wounding and/or overestimated our relationship bond.

The core of Laura's treatment involves early failures of basic trust in her primary relationships. I am reminded that trust is the deepest connection and an evolving process. There is also her guilt and shame that about continuing this relationship with Alex. Laura is now willing to come out of hiding.

I wonder and ask if she saw him. Laura responds, "No. We agreed that he could call in the future and I would answer, but I wouldn't be able to talk. He made several calls. I would answer. We didn't talk."

I ask, "No words, just rings as a signal?"

"Yes. We held the silence and, of course, the tension. We are both married to people we care deeply about. We love our spouses. We both have children." As she answers I understand that this is a fragile thread of unbearable love and memory. Their feelings are felt and transmitted in time and space, once through a transatlantic cable beneath the ocean, now though the invisible ethers. This exchange was in code, an S.O.S. or perhaps a distress call?

"He traveled to Northern Canada near the tundra on a work project. I dreamed about him but, no, we didn't meet." I ask, "Do you remember the dream?" Laura leafs back through her dream notebook and reads,

> Dream: *A snow scene in a frozen landscape with something, a large creature, moving beneath the snow, tunneling under the snow. At some point it bursts through. It's a beautiful silver-colored fox.*

Laura focuses on the scene, the beautiful animal, and its crafty, surprising way of moving. I remind her that Alex had been on this continent. "Laura," I say, "through the frozen emotional atmosphere you have been feeling for a long time, an animal bursts up through the snow, your instinctual energy is moving below the surface. Perhaps it is hunting, hungry? It not only rises, it bursts from below the surface. It is a beautiful, magical creature. It is alive, making itself known."

Laura says, "Yes, of course it must be related to Alex coming up out of nowhere in my life." I wondered to myself if Alex was her "silver fox," her handsome older man. "The dream creature is a sly trickster or guide. A silver animal is highly unusual creature. Silver is valuable, reflective, dazzling, " I say.

Again I see the dream motif of "*unseen then seen*" like the earlier eagle dream.

The dynamic and painful tension of the first and subsequent calls from Alex in the early months of Laura's therapy now opens a floodgate of unfrozen feelings. Laura expresses unresolved loss *and* guilt for having any interest in another man who is not her husband. Laura is finally turning to help, something she had been circling for a long time. She is taking the risk of bursting through the winter of her emotional life.

Out of consciously bearing suffering and tension, a profound relationship with her Self, her soul is being born anew. In other words, she held the emotional tension rather than acting out. We never know ahead of time what can emerge if we bear the tension of waiting. She loves this man and she loves her husband.

The emergent possibility becomes the unexpected third possibility, here symbolized by the fox, a wild vibrant, beautiful, animal, not one man or the other, but a different choice, a symbol of Self. By turning her attention and energy inward and honestly owning herself as a woman, her history and her dreams; she is creatively choosing a path that offers the containment of an analytic relationship. She seems to be choosing herself. The silver fox is part of Laura's emergent, visible soul.

The analysis moves on intensively week after week. Due to her long commute I arrange for extended sessions in late afternoon and the following morning. Laura continues to share her childhood memories and voice her neglected needs. She moves into and through many emotional experiences, and reports feeling relief while in sessions. I note to myself that she is often home alone while Eugene is away working out of town.

Laura says she is speaking with family and friends with more honesty and is realizing how hard it is for her to say "no" to others' demands and requests. She literally practices interactions and saying "no" to others by role-playing with me and at home using an audio recorder. I encourage her to create a dance with her aggressive energy, which she does at home alone, too shy or afraid to share this in person. She seeks and begins attending a class. "I found an African dance class with a wonderful woman teacher," she says. "I can just be me, moving alone in a group with drumming music. I can feel my belly, my body, these are really good feelings." New experiences and new people are refreshing and revitalizing to her life.

Dreams continue. She records them with self-discipline.

In any one session of Laura's analysis, we talk about many feelings, dreams, many relationships, and stories of the present and the past.

CHAPTER 9

Finding the Baby

A succession or series of dreams focusing on a baby, or babies, emerges over time.

The reoccurring theme is the quality of care and the nourishment of an infant, especially involving her capacity to breast-feed.

One year into the analysis:

Dream: *I was nursing a baby, a malnourished one, and was able to provide the needed nourishment even though I thought I was too old to produce breast milk.*

One-and-a-half years into the analysis:

Dream: 8 a.m. I am in a nursery with some other women. We're looking after the babies who are sleeping on several massage tables covered with white sheets. The tables have been pushed together so that there is broad expanse of surface area.

The babies are newborn so they can all be left on the tabletops without being in danger of falling off. The women are coming and going, taking turns watching the babies. At one point I see that one of the babies has wiggled over toward one of the cracks between the tables. I lift up the sheet covering the baby and hand the baby back to the mother, with a caution about the baby getting caught in the crack. The mother is very grateful and puts the baby back in the center of the table.

Soon after that, almost all the mothers have left with all the babies. There is one baby left on the table. I notice that after awhile the sleeping baby has moved toward one of the cracks between the tables. It is a little girl and her head is caught, face down. I go to her and lift her in my arms. It's the first time I have seen this baby. She is extremely small. Her head is no larger than my fist. She is wrapped in a soft, white flannel cloth that covers her head. I pull back the cloth from her face, saying to the other women, "Look at her. See how beautiful she is. She looks familiar, with dark hair." The baby scrunches up her face and moves her mouth as if she's hungry. Her mother isn't in the room and I have the impulse to hold the baby to my breast and nurse her. I know I could do that, but I hesitate, thinking, "Maybe the mother wouldn't want me to do that. Maybe my milk is not safe because of my having hepatitis." This makes me feel terrible disappointment, but the mother comes back, the baby gets fed, and I caution all the mothers about those cracks between the tables.

"Even in my dreams I fear that I may contaminate others. I'm not safe enough. My milk is not safe enough to nourish a baby, a new life," she says. Diagnosed with breast cancer and hepatitis B and C in her twenties, she experiences feeling marginalized socially. She sees herself as physically disfigured and emotionally wounded by illness and disease. She felt shame for having the illness of cancer and loss of her breast was followed by a sense of failure, ugliness, and self-rejection. Like so many others, she finds it difficult to make sense of her illnesses. "Have I caused this somehow? Is it some kind of divine punishment?" Emotionally and physically she fell through the cracks in childhood. She felt that again in her twenties, no one saw her; no one screened the contaminated blood that infected her during mastectomy surgery.

Two-and-a-half years into the analysis:

Dream: I come upon an older woman whose mother has died. She is overcome with grief. I can think of no other way to comfort her but to offer her my breast. She nurses hungrily while I explain to some other women that I can do this even though I have only one breast and even though the woman is so old. "See!" I say, pointing to the woman, "I have wrapped her in a blanket. She is warm and comforted. It's working just fine."

Laura reflects: "I'm taking the grieving and hungry part of myself to my own breast. The one breast will have to be enough. I'm defending myself against the possible criticism and lack of faith of the other women. Could the older woman be my mother?" After a long pause she says, "I feel that my mother was emotionally needy, and the 'she' in the dream really could be me."

I answer, "You are engaged in what might seem impossible, unacceptable, and even shocking. You are actively determining what is needed in the moment. In the presence of such profound grief, you can think of no better way. Offering one's breast is an instinctual, primal biological impulse with an infant. Here, this offering is symbolic; you offer your breast to a bereft and vulnerable woman. You hold her close to your heart. You swaddle this older grieving woman; she is the daughter of a deceased mother. She is full of sorrow and hunger. You bring her toward your heart and feed the hunger of her entire being, keeping her warm and containing her fully. This is the compassion of one woman to another, a mother to a daughter, and a daughter to an elder mother." I pause for her to catch up with my reflections and continue, "Laura, you are a daughter who has lost her mother. You are a mother who lost her first pregnancy. Your mother lost her mother, and so on. The deepest biological connection is between a mother and her child, and at some point, must be surrendered." I am telling Laura that in this dream she is accepting and taking responsibility for the care of her own grief, for herself. What has been wounded in the feminine has to be healed in the feminine.

I understand that Laura is able to psychologically use me as a mother figure. She is "projecting" this feeling onto the analysis and me. This is a positive "transference". She is symbolically and emotionally held with care and fed emotionally, spiritually. She is learning to feed herself by taking this time to honor her dreams, feelings, and reflections on her life in a safe setting.

Four years into the analysis:

Dream: I am sitting beside a young man. We are both in our youth, our twenties. Something extraordinary has happened-maybe even cataclysmic-and we are left to care for the life that is left on earth-to nurture the young animals remaining. I look to my left toward the young man and hand him an infant. He holds it to his breast and the baby immediately puts its mouth on the man's breast and starts nursing. I am amazed and thrilled to see that this is possible. I say, "I didn't know that you could do that but I see how natural it seems." The young man takes this completely in stride. I then take another creature in my arms. I look down into the baby's face and see that it has the trunk of a miniature elephant. It is a tiny elephant. The trunk moves immediately to my right breast (or where it used to be), reaching through the white shirt I'm wearing. I think, "Look how well this is working. It really helps to have a trunk."

"My feeling in this dream," Laura says, "is we are all survivors and we are charged with structuring a new way to be in life. The new life will be completely different from whatever we have known before. In both cases, the young man's and mine, the nurturing person doesn't have to have a female breast. All humans can nurture the young of all species."

I sense her focusing more on how to creatively move on in life after enormous upheaval.

In this fourth dream of the baby series, we discuss how Laura can nourish her self. What, who, is the baby elephant? We can see how she can offer nourishment from both the masculine and feminine aspects of herself. She transcends old beliefs about the way life "should" be. I note that in the dream, she might have a new right breast, replacing the one she lost to cancer and surgery. The diseased breast is replaced. Perhaps she "grew" or regenerated a breast that is healthy enough to feed an infant. This is wish fulfillment on her part, compensation for the harsh reality. Yet in the realm of the unconscious psyche this transformation or healing is symbolically possible.

The baby elephant represented her orphaned instinctual life. This is a wild creature, not domesticated like a companion dog. This wild animal energy has the potential of becoming something much, much bigger, more extraordinary. Symbolically elephants[10] are archetypally divine creatures in Buddhist and Hindu mythology. The impulse, consciously and unconsciously, to nourish divine instinct is very important.

Listening to this dream I hear a profound and successful drive toward integration in Laura's psyche. She and a sensitive, generous young man are working cooperatively and acknowledging the interdependence of living species. He is an aspect of her inner masculine capacities, the animus. Here, he is integrated: full of youthful energy *and* maternal capacity. She accepts him as part of herself that is capable of nourishing her instinctual life. The archetype of the infant, or baby, carries the developing sense of the future or "futurity" and creativity. Something new has arrived, is developing, and life carries on in the face of cataclysmic events.

Over time Laura and I continue to follow the amplification of such symbols raising, amplifying them to broader and deeper collective understanding. Universal stories: myths, folktales, and fairy tales are rooted in the timeless archetypal realm of the psyche. The deeper unconscious is further away from personal, biographic life and personality conflicts. Laura's feelings, memories, and personal associations must be attended to first, then we amplify symbols, stories, and themes find the deeper universal meanings.

CHAPTER 10

Medical Trauma and Illness

I ask questions throughout our sessions, "Where do you feel this in your body now?"

"Tell me about the time when you realized that."

"What were you feeling, seeing, and hearing?"

Sensory and physical awareness grounds the analysis in and through Laura's body and my body. Although we use or apply intellect, this work is not an intellectual exercise. This is a metaphoric process better described as cooking, involving intuition and senses. Images and themes are symbolic ingredients. There is the vessel of the analytic relationship, and there is heat from emotional tension within Laura. Sometimes there's heat between us, excitement, energy, sometimes, though rarely, anger. The greater difficulty is the tension within Laura as she withholds her feelings or awareness of the deeper truth of what happened in the past or what could becoming. She is beginning to consciously experience the emotion. The heat of experienced emotion allows the process of "cooking" the raw experiences of her life. This "food" is nourishing to Laura's soul. "The meaning of my life feels greater, richer, when I can really feel and think about my dreams and memories," Laura reflects. " I remember the beautiful, tender feeling of holding Karen in my arms when she was a newborn. Nursing her was one of the most deeply satisfying experiences of my life. Even though I lost one of my breasts later, I can remember." Feelings are held in her mind and body, accessible when she has the space and safety. It's a slow cooking process allowing deeper integration, deeper strengthening of the ego and the ego's connection with the greater Self.

Learning how to access memories, identify bodily feelings, and find words to express this is a true challenge. Out of the darkness of Laura's depression and sorrow, we both observe that her capacity for self-reflection is increasing. Using the metaphor of cooking and alchemy, Laura's unconscious "leaden" feeling is slowly being transformed into the gold of consciousness, a sense of lightness in body and mind.

Her tears are part of the purification. A healthy attachment to me as her therapist/analyst is reparative.

In analytic psychology, the infant or baby in dreams points to the archetype of the Divine Child within the Self. A second, or symbolic rebirth within is underway. Laura is now living a life increasingly informed by her dreams, the symbolic expressions of the psyche. She lives in both the physical material world and the inner world of spirit and imagination. Laura, like most artists, has an easier access to imagination and feels compelled to express her inner experience. The baby is a symbol of new life, creativity, and potential or future. 'Baby' can also represent our infantile, regressive ways and feelings. Laura's dream of the *baby falling between the cracks* is about a neglected, unseen, and unprotected baby. This surely describes her emotional experience, though not necessarily an actual event. In our therapeutic work together we attempt to differentiate new life from her former dysfunctional, regressive expressions.

In the course of our work, Laura slowly shares her experience of bodily damage, shame, and fear of her incapacity to nourish with her milk. Through dreams her psyche is allowing her to nurse her Self, her own hunger for love, her grief as a motherless woman, and her animal instincts damaged by cataclysm. Laura begins to claim her capacity to make and share "milk," the symbolic form of love produced mysteriously within her body. It flows, circulating within and out to others, nourishing her relationships with friends, family, and the larger world. In analyzing her dream, Laura is progressing toward self-healing from within.

The series of baby dreams is giving Laura and me a deeper glimpse into the development of her early history. Laura's particular challenges involve emotional neglect in infancy and childhood. There are few memories of the period of time before, during, and after of her mother's hospitalization for a "nervous breakdown." Laura was three years old. Her father's ceaseless work and, she later realized, marital infidelity kept him away from home. Laura remembers a nightmare from childhood:

Fear of becoming disembodied, of bodily disintegration.

These early losses are compounded with a late miscarriage in her first pregnancy at age twenty. About seven years later after giving birth to her two children she is diagnosed with advanced breast cancer. She was treated with a radical mastectomy and cobalt radiation, *and* coincidentally, accidentally being infected by the hospital staff, with liver diseases. During this same period there were a series of sudden losses: her mother, father, and grandmother. All her most significant attachment figures died. Both parents, mother first, died suddenly from heart attacks. There were no funerals or memorials. A decade later Laura suffers the mental crisis and suicide attempt of her oldest child, seventeen-year-old Karen who is diagnosed as schizophrenic.

For very good reasons, the baby, the new life within my patient Laura, is very hungry, very frightened, and very angry.

During the analysis there is good news: Laura is reestablishing a warm and regular relationship with her oldest, most significant woman friend, Emma who had been living in Asia for years and has now has returned to live in New England near Laura. Emma was experiencing trials within her own marriage and moved into a tiny home with an art studio nearby. Laura and I celebrate this new development and renewed emotional support.

The wounds in Laura's body, heart, and mind truly bleed into every aspect of her life.

She is now working with and slowly accepting this reality: *compounded traumatic and chronic loss* has filled so many of her years.

Suffering is a core truth of the human condition. The way of becoming an authentic human being demands the acceptance of the suffering that we meet in life. Unless we embrace and integrate this reality, true joy and true liberation remain elusive.

CHAPTER 11

Amelia the Guardian

Almost three years have passed since we began the analysis.

Many patients have very limited access to childhood memories; a few say they cannot remember anything. I am finding that Laura has slowly accessed a rich storehouse of childhood memories.

She feels that her parents a wanted another baby; they wanted her. She remembers the nickname her father used when she was very young: "Muffin". She reports early, vague, memories from the time of her mother's hospitalization due to a "nervous condition," an emotional breakdown of unspecified severity. As a three-year-old Laura was left in the care of "a woman" for an unspecified period of time while other family members were away.

World War II deeply affected Laura's life. There were years of absent fathering and financial strains that led to taking boarders into the home. She remembers the air-raid preparations and covering windows for the blackouts. Laura spoke of the moves and her memories of her mother trying hard to create a home at every military post. The family, then just Laura and her mother, moved frequently to accommodate her father's military service. Her brother George was much older and away at school. "When my father was physically present, my mother expressed her frustration that he was gone frequently and wasn't emotionally available to her. Laura says, "I heard her pleading, saw her pounding on his back. She hit him in front of me. I was eight years old and remember this clearly." Once in her early adulthood Laura had begun to understand more fully how unsatisfying the marriage was to her mother.

As a very young child she spent time alone in nature. She remembers this play and exploration as enjoyable. There was one remembered playmate, a little girl named Caroline who lived nearby in one of the many places Laura had lived. She had happy memories of being with her mother in the country, exploring nature together. She remembers her mother's capacity to make things with her hands.

Laura arrives for her next analytic session.

She enters my office carrying a large old cardboard box in her arms and says, "This week I found my very special box containing my doll Amelia and all her clothing."

Laura describes herself as "saving things to a fault." Boxes of "saved things" traveled from the east coast to the west coast and back to the east coast. The war years, filled with shortages and frugal practices, were deeply impressed in Laura's psyche. After years, many of these boxes are still unpacked. This particular box in her library/storage room recently caught Laura's attention. Many years had passed since this box was opened.

She relates this story to me: "When I was eight, Mother and I were living alone on a military base in Massachusetts. My brother George was twelve years older than me and after attending college he was working in Chicago. My father was traveling for his military work. He was away a great deal of the time. My mother kept me out of school for the entire year." I ask, "Why?" "I was told that I had pneumonia," Laura continues. "The unspoken reason was to ease my mother's loneliness. My maternal grandmother had died the year before. Later I realized that my father, who frequently traveled with his secretary, was having an affair."

During Laura's year on the military base when she was kept out of school, her mother made a doll that Laura named "Amelia". Her mother also created and sewed a complete a wardrobe of doll clothes.

She remembers, "I'm sitting cross-legged on the floor in the middle of the little living room. I cut through the patterned cotton fabric with my small scissors. I'm making and tailoring costumes from scraps left by my mother. The garments are for Amelia, my doll. I'm eight years old and I say my doll Amelia is two years old. My mother had made my doll by hand. I remember that it felt like an eternity until she was complete. Mother made Amelia her first dress; it was a smock of green gingham.

"Outside, the days without school wash by, I have no idea how many days or months. I clip, sew, and arrange pieces of fabric over and over. I look through my mother's glossy magazines. I'm drawn to the glamorous women who are smiling, striding across stages or down stairs in long skirts like Loretta Young (the actress) or riding horses, driving cars, or dancing. They're always going somewhere and having a good time, meeting someone, always getting ready for a dance partner. Amelia sits watching my every move. She's my friend, my protector, my little sister, and the one I confide in."

Several years prior to living on the military base, Laura and her mother had been living together in a small room at a New England boarding school dormitory, where her mother became surrogate parent to twenty "sent away" wealthy daughters of others. Laura's father was traveling for military business and her brother George was away at school.

"I stole pink fabric from another girl's kindergarten cubbyhole at the boarding school," says Laura. "It was one thing I couldn't resist, the cloth felt cool and slippery. I can still feel it. It felt magic to me. It almost made a song and was the color of a princess's ball gown. The beautiful pink satin seemed to say to me, "I am a life of beauty and happiness, I belong to you."

"That was my first crime," Laura says. Later that day, when her mother discovered that Laura had taken the pink fabric, her mother's hand delivered a swift, stinging blow across Laura's face. The attraction had proved too much for a six-year-old, sad little girl. The fabric had possessed her. It represented a life she did not have; it represented other, more charming, imagined possibilities.

Laura returns to her story of the doll, the clothes, and time away from school while living on the military base. Her mother allowed her to go to the small movie theater there. Laura doesn't mention other playmates on the base. She immersed herself in the dreamy ideal world of Hollywood's fantasies. That was when Laura began to sew, stitching her doll's clothes and fantasizing life as an artist in fabric and costume design.

Child's play, such as the love of cloth, exploring its possibilities, can be a portal, a sign, a key to the future and, here with me in her session, a bridge to memories of the past. For Laura, this was the official beginning of handwork that would eventually carry her to New York City and Japan, allowing her into the hearts of others with her precious handmade clothing and gifts.

Fear lingered in the background for Laura during World War II. Many people felt this fear; it was especially true in military families. By age eight, during the daytime, she found a creative way to cope. She became absorbed in creating doll clothes, dressing and directing characters in her made up stories and, by night, in the blackout years, sitting at the window in her darkened bedroom watching the stars until her mother covered the window. She wondered who might live there? And how far away was the future?

We talk more about the doll, her earlier childhood, when her grandmother lived with them, and the war years with blackouts, curfews, limited food, shortages of supplies of basic things of life, and the time that they needed to take in boarders to make ends meet. These were daily concerns. As she discusses the "difficult years," together, we translate this to her "profoundly lonely years."

Laura lifts the doll out of the box to show me. I touch it gently. Its body is soft; the limbs are those of a rag doll. Amelia's eternally young face is painted in a permanent gentle smile. Amelia is a one-of-a-kind gift and a rare treasure.

The doll Amelia rests in Laura's hands now and helps her tell the story of the stolen pink satin and her mother's anger and her sadness in those years. Amelia was beautifully created by her mother and provided a companion for her, a lonely little girl. Laura sees that creativity can be expressed, or "born," out of a loving intention, as Amelia was, and she also knows that creativity can be the expression of many other emotions: suffering, grief, loneliness, anger, and fear.

Laura tenderly lifts garment after garment out of the old cardboard box, taking time to remember the past. Her tears fall as Amelia's presence acts as a bridge to her childhood memories. Over the prior week Laura had carefully hand washed and ironed each piece of clothing, taking time to remember and reflect. The delicately stitched and smocked dresses, belted coats, trousers for playing, hats, and even mittens; they are all here. The fabrics ranged from age-yellowed sheer gauze, red-and-white checkered cotton, brown corduroy, and green gingham, to blue wool from her mother's old coat. The forms and fabric hold the shape, the truth, and the substance of Laura's dreams and stories. Amelia still holds Laura's heart.

Early childhood was a time of several surgeries that Laura describes as "horrific and painful". She feels the adults had failed to prepare and protect her from confusion, fear, and great pain. "I felt frightened, angry, betrayed." One memory from age six is of being carried upstairs in a building to have her tonsils removed. "I tried telling the doctor and nurses that I hurt, I felt everything!" The anesthesia didn't work for her and her screams were ignored. "Someone crushed their body onto mine to hold my arms and legs down to keep me from kicking," she says.

She shares another memory, one from early adolescence. She had emergency abdominal surgery for appendicitis; again this operation involved a lack of adequate anesthesia. Her father was at the hospital and didn't intervene; he did not protect her by communicating to the doctor about her prior issues with anesthesia.

She arranged an additional analytic session when her brother George was visiting Boston. He accepted Laura's invitation to attend the session. At that time he was over seventy years old. He was a gentleman, more formal than Laura. She wanted to talk together explicitly about early childhood memories. In discussion with her before the session he shared a shocking revelation that he had known about for years but never told Laura. George repeats in the session, "When you called to ask me to come to your session to discuss your childhood, I remembered that when you were just a little baby you went to the hospital. I was about twelve or thirteen and remembered that mother spoke about it. You'd had a respiratory illness. Your thymus gland was irradiated. Apparently in the 1930s radiation directed to the enlarged thymus gland in infancy was thought by some medical doctors to reduce the occurrence of certain early childhood illness." Laura says, "In those years radiation practices were surely more primitive and less modulated in strength." Laura speculates, "The early onset of my breast cancer in my twenties might be related to the radiation exposure I had when I was an infant. That treatment may have damaged my thymus gland. We now know that the this gland's function is important to the immune system." Laura expresses her appreciation for George's visit and his recall of this dismaying information.

In a later session when he is not present she vents her utter frustration and anger that he remembered this important fact so late in her life, and expresses anger toward her parents and doctors who subjected her tiny innocent body to a treatment so poorly understood.

As a result of breast cancer surgery and cobalt radiation treatment, Laura suffered physical pain and profound loss of physical integrity caused by the disease. The emotional pain of chronic self doubt and shame followed. The disfigurement and mutilation of a radical mastectomy, the surgical choice of the 1950s was, in Laura's words, "devastating." For her the surgery was immediately followed liver damage caused by hepatitis B and C infections by the hospital's errors. Laura suffered a severe narcissistic wound to her ego and her persona, changing the course of her life just at the height of Laura's physical beauty and fertility.

Throughout our sessions together, Laura ventilates years of repressed anger and sorrow. Outside of our sessions she works to empower herself by writing, researching information, and discussing some of these memories with her family and friends.

Laura's unexpressed rage from numerous experiences: early surgical procedures without adequate anesthesia, cancer, body disfigurement, and the hospital's inadvertent infection with hepatitis B and C, the sudden losses of her parents and her profoundly disappointing marital circumstances; these emotional events merge into a deep mistrust of many authority figures, especially doctors, and, many males.

Laura's innate sense of divine order, divine compassion, the right-
ness in the universe, was deeply shaken in her life. She searches within
for a new order to emerge from the chaos and finds some comfort and
security in the natural world. Her doll Amelia now has a place on a
shelf over her bed. Laura makes a miniature breastplate, a shield, and
places it over the doll's chest, heart. Laura says, "She's a warrior."

CHAPTER 12

New Worlds

The following year.

As the time approached for my long-planned move to Santa Fe, New Mexico I suggest that Laura consider continuing her analytic work with a analyst who lives physically closer to her in New England. After consideration of a good match for her needs, I provide her with a name of a mature, respected female colleague who is well versed in Jung's psychology and works with the body. She lives in Western Massachusetts. I do not push Laura to make a decision. I feel she needs to be free to choose what she needs. Although appreciative of my suggestion, Laura declines working with a new analyst. The choice always remains open, if she wishes to continue with an analyst closer to her home for face-to-face therapeutic work weekly.

Laura expresses sadness that the time is nearing when I will move. We share our mutual concerns about the future of our analytic relationship and wonder how it will be to live far apart, and continue our therapeutic work. I too express my sadness about the loss of our weekly face-to-face relationship.

In the outset of her analysis we had discussed how we could continue when I moved. Laura asks, "Is it possible that we could continue by phone?" This was not something I'd done before so was less familiar with the pros and cons. I had already planned to travel to Boston regularly, four times a year, once a season, to continue to see a few patients, friends, and colleagues. Laura was one of my patients that I'd see intensively during each of those four weeks.

We had created a well-established and productive relationship. I was willing to try weekly phone sessions to see if this felt safe, productive and satisfying along with the seasonal intensive sessions in person.

Laura also plans to visit me for face-to-face sessions in Santa Fe. Having been to this area before, she is aware that there is much to explore. Her interest in art and textiles and the cultures of the Southwest offered rich resources: museums and research facilities in Santa Fe. I shared my hope that she will visit me.

I take time off from all work for the relocation of my family's life.

Once in Santa Fe I am initially preoccupied with resettling my family, helping my sons to begin in their new schools, and establishing a community of colleagues and friends. I construct a schedule for regular travel to Boston. Laura confirms plans to use the weeks I am visiting for intensive work with me, arranging a number of face-to-face sessions in each of my week visits.

I am not sure yet if the Southwest will really become permanent home. Its high desert ecology is so far from the ocean, which has been so important in my life. Santa Fe is a very small city with tri-cultural and tri-racial richness (Hispanic, Native American, and Anglo) and complexity. Prior to our move my husband, a child psychologist, was offered employment as a psychologist with the public schools. He was looking forward to his work as a bi-lingual child and family psychologist serving Hispanic, Native American, and Anglo populations. He is fluent in Spanish and had served in the Peace Corps in Colombia, South America.

I am looking forward to my children having another culturally diverse experience of life. They were born and attended elementary school in a racially and culturally diverse community just north of Boston. I have my family to tend, friends to reconnect with, new colleagues to meet, and my own life to explore. Professional therapists must nourish their lives, live as fully as possible, and find collegial support. It is a challenging and rich time of life.

The seasonal visiting and working in Boston is a pleasure to me. When there, I spend time working with patients and enjoying relationships with valued friends, family, and colleagues. I hike in nature, visit the ocean.

The deep relational bonds developed through hard work over time with patients, including Laura, are secure. Between my trips to Boston Laura and I continue our weekly analytic sessions by phone.

She joined her husband on a long, important business trip to Japan. When we resume our therapeutic work by phone she says, "It was wonderful. The Japanese are inspiring artists and artisans. They love wood. It's in their craftsmanship and architecture, especially the historic buildings. Their printmaking and textile design is exquisite, detailed and balanced. The cultural appreciation of arts and crafts is palpable." The couple took time away from business to explore the countryside. This was unusual. It seems that they enjoyed the trip together and that Laura was very moved by the entire experience. She has long expressed a deep an interest in Japanese culture and religion. She was interested in World War II, especially how the Japanese people endured the catastrophic devastation following the bombings of Hiroshima and Nagasaki. How they faced the tragedies and mourned in order to resume life was deeply meaningful to her.

She had a fall while traveling. She shared, "I tripped on stone steps injuring my knee. It wasn't too bad." Laura, now in her early sixties, seems very fit and agile. In the years I've known her she's never reported a fall or any illness. In a passing thought I wondered to myself if she was overtired or somehow out of balance?

She has been aware of the possibility of reoccurrence of cancer since her diagnosis and treatment in her twenties. In remission for forty years, she attempts to prevent that possibility by being proactive about her health. She cultivates a healthy lifestyle and reads a great deal. "I follow current cancer research", Laura says, "I pay attention to my diet and eat mostly vegetables, some rice, nuts and fruit. I eat very little red meat these days. We eat out less. Oh! And I cut out sugar, that's very important. Sometimes Eugene joins me on my daily walks in woods." She talks about the yoga class she joined; a new community of friends has developed around this practice. She has also begun regular treatments with an acupuncturist, has a weekly massage, and has occasional chiropractic adjustments.

She is relying on a variety of supportive health care practitioners and connecting more to her local community. She is expressing pleasure about this and it's clear that her depression has lifted somewhat.

I still wonder about the fall.

CHAPTER 13

Catastrophes and the Failure of Fantasies

Much like turtles who carry their house on their back, we carry our personal history with us our entire lives. Our history is integral to our very being, even though it is likely that we are unaware of much detail or the depth in the patterns we learned in our very early years. Family dynamics are fateful in that we are born each into specific circumstances that have profound personal effects. How we face and struggle with our given life situation is a core determinant of our life's course.

Over the years several of Laura's dreams had a theme of a catastrophic situation and aftermath. In her initial dream there is a vast and lonely landscape, stillness with no action, no living creatures. In a later dream there is catastrophe although she is no longer alone, someone is at her side and she is actively assisting the next generation. My understanding continues to evolve over time. Every patient spirals back and forth between their history to the present; they remember more, adding detail and substance as well as bringing their current more mature vision to their life story. Certainly this was true for Laura.

Laura grew up in a difficult emotional atmosphere and with the model of her parents' dissatisfactory marriage. She also was told and observed the challenging effects of her maternal grandmother's unhappy marriage. She tells me the family history that she knows: "In the 1930s, my maternal grandmother, "Nonny" lived with us in my early childhood home after her marriage ended in a divorce." It was unusual in the 1920s that a woman, the wife, would initiate a divorce. Her grandmother did not remarry. Laura says, "In her childhood, my mother had lived alone with her mother. In those days divorce was unusual and viewed as shameful and suspicious, especially for a woman." She idealized her grandmother who was an artist. Laura's maternal family was very small. She never met her maternal grandfather and didn't have extended family support. Laura's mother suffered severe depression and was hospitalized for depression, "nervous breakdown". Grandmother Nonny, Laura's mother, and granddaughter Laura, these three generations of women were emotionally involved and interdependent until

Nonny died when Laura was seven. Her father was frequently away from home due to work and an extramarital affair that lasted for years.

The models for Laura's adult marital intimacy were three generations of unhappy marriages, and men, husbands and fathers, who were distant physically and emotionally, from their children.

In her first marriage Laura felt victimized, overworked and under acknowledged. The fantasy she had of "a happy marriage and an involved, emotionally invested husband and father for her children," failed. Her in-laws proved to be overly involved and needy in many ways, and her first husband had an affair. Laura came to see that the pattern of her first marriage was similar to her parents' marriage, "My husband was emotionally unavailable and had an affair when I needed him most–during my illness," says Laura.

Her mother died suddenly when she was twenty, followed by her father's sudden death a few years later. These unprocessed traumatic losses affected her marriage negatively in a number of ways: loss of extended family support physically and emotionally; loss of normal bereavement which contributed to depression; and the demanding psychological reorientation to life following the death of both parents, especially early in adulthood.

For Laura, loss and fear of abandonment remain significant the psychological issues that she carried unconsciously into her marriages and intimate relationships. In our analytic work Laura is successfully working on making these issues more conscious.

In her second marriage, she and Eugene began with an exciting professional partnership. With their blended families and severe crises in the children's lives, the emotional and financial demands had been overwhelmingly stressful. What she had been seeing over the years, and is more concerned about now, is Eugene's preoccupation with creative projects, his lack of emotional availability, and his absences from home due to work. She discusses the similarity between her father and Eugene. If she has concerns or fears of his infidelity, she is not ready, or cannot, talk about this in her sessions.

Though the work Eugene orchestrated in the scientific field was fulfilling to him, their lives were also affected negatively by the chaos created by major projects. "They involved tremendous financial pressures, endless hours of work away from home, constant deadlines, a voluminous number of business meetings, and the necessity of coping with and directing teams of people," says Laura. Success came later, "Yes there was financial relief, but not without cost to our intimacy," she says. She has some regret that she surrendered her priorities to his professional projects. "I, myself, and the world saw my work as "less important," Laura adds, "I'm not really a public person and I'm ambivalent about getting too much attention. Quite a bind." She realizes that professional oversights and lack of acknowledgement of her professional contributions to projects have been painful blows to her self-esteem. She is angry but has not confronted her husband. She is still avoiding this conflict.

Living in the shadow of her husband's success was emotionally mixed for her. "When we moved away from the urban life in Palo Alto to a more rural setting in Vermont, we both felt physically and emotionally relieved, better, more free." Laura adds, "I feel more rooted in this familiar world of nature." Separating from a highly urban setting reduced their stress significantly. Their pace of life at that time did not allow for reflection. Conscious change requires reflection. In analysis, Laura is realizing that she fails herself in her life with her own passive acceptance of situations, such as not insisting on recognition by her husband, or avoiding making decisions about what she wants and actually asking for it.

She consciously decides to leave the bed she had shared with her husband to sleep in another room in the house. I assume both Laura and Eugene act in self-protective ways. They have not been fully aware of how their behaviors create increased stress in their intimate life with each other. "Laura," I say, "it is important for you to recognize your own passive and aggressive anger, such as moving out of the bedroom, without a through and honest conversation with Eugene. That a form of acting-out in your marriage."

During this period of the analysis she has many dreams with this theme:

It's night and I'm traveling with Eugene, become separated from him, and am trying to find my way back to our meeting place, trying to find the key I've misplaced.

Laura's fear of openly expressing anger toward men is rooted deeply in her personal and the collective experience as a woman. Laura's anger toward her father, her former and current husbands, bosses, medical personnel, her mother, and various family members was not openly expressed. She is angry that the "divine" has allowed unfair, critical losses in her life such as her cancer. Painful obstacles in her life, especially her daughter's illness, haunt her. She continues to struggle with her personal guilt over the course of her children's lives.

What Laura is *not yet* discussing is the latent disease of hepatitis C. She doesn't report discussing fear over the future of her health and life with Eugene, but I know they are both aware of this. As the analysis progresses Laura takes our discussion of her passive and aggressive behavior seriously. She becomes more active in her life by participating in her daughter's mental health care and living situation. She hires a personal caretaker for Karen's care and arranges an expert medical review. This decision relieves her of responsibility, some travel, and a great deal of anxiety. She reads, stays informed, on the current research in schizophrenia and joins the National Alliance for Mental Health (NAMI). Laura engages in more social relationships and spends more time with her friend Emma. She worries about Emma and Eugene's high blood pressure, poor diets and little exercise. Though true concerns, she is still projecting her medical worries onto others.

Laura now begins to redirect her anger and plunges into a creative surge of her own making. She finally makes time to design her own art studio and start new projects. Eugene is highly supportive of building the studio and her creative expression. She drew plans with the help of a local architect. They find a local builder and work commences. Laura also seeks a weaving teacher invites Emma to join the weaving class with her. Both enjoy this new form of art and extended time together. Laura creates and weaves several rugs; one is primarily red with a golden Phoenix in the center. Her second rug is darker tones with images of loons will be for her studio. She finds an excellent etching, typesetting, and printing teacher. Laura designs and creates a series of books including etchings and poetry from her dreams. Eugene encourages her to have an exhibition. She agrees to show a few things in a small local venue.

She takes photos of her on-going projects and shares them with me in person on my trips to Boston or sends them via mail. Her pride and enjoyment in this flow of creative work is evident. She is blossoming and really enjoying her life.

Laura says, "We are making more time to enjoy nature together here." They have a small boat, a "putt, putt" with quiet little motor for floating on the local ponds near their Vermont home. She describes her most cherished yearly trip in late summer: a retreat and renewal in wilderness, an important part of the couple's intimate relationship. They travel to a remote primitive camp on a little island in Newfoundland. It can be reached only by boat. For years a Native American guide meets them at the dock of a remote village. He brings a canoe and paddles, helps them unload their rental car, and load their supplies into their wooden canoe. He has become a friend over the years advising them on weather and water conditions and exchanging news of their families. Laura and Eugene had met his wife and children and were interested in news about the issues in the local Native community. They board the canoe and paddle to a small island with a primitive building. They settle the supplies, make up a rustic bed, and build a fire. No work, no telephones. Their guide -friend will come to check on them every few days. Every day they paddle around the little island staying close to the shoreline communing with wild creatures. "When I am living there, I feel heaven on earth," says Laura, "Gene and I find refuge and restore our sanity in this natural world. This is our pilgrimage into the wilderness." For a couple that does not find solace in attending traditional religious services, this retreat is essential and nourishing for their souls.

The family used to come to their remote camp when the children were younger, not anymore. Laura and Eugene are now beginning to talk more openly and acknowledge their need to think of a future that allows them both more freedom from responsibilities. The various major crises of their children, now adults, have calmed down. Their lives seem to have "normalized," at least briefly.

Laura tends emotional bonds with her very small extended family, a few cousins and her brother George, now seventy-six years old, who lives with his wife Clara in Ashville, North Carolina. Although there is a surface sense of normality in the marriage and extended family, the deeper issues of Laura's future health and Eugene's inability to disengage from a pattern of overwork and absence from home linger in the background. Laura and Eugene are not engaged with me or any other therapist to get help in addressing ongoing issues.

With their move from Palo Alto to Vermont some years ago, Eugene committed to less work away but that did not happen. He continued to attend regular business meetings in New York, New Mexico, Europe, and Asia. Again he is spending increasingly more time away from home working on creative projects. She is disappointed and beginning to speak directly with him about her feelings. This is an important change.

CHAPTER 14

Guilt and Secrets

Karen lives in a halfway house across the country. Laura arranged this and contributes ongoing financial support. After a number of years of trying to coordinate from a distance, Laura hired a private social worker, Jeanne Howe, to supervise Karen's treatment program, make medical appointments, and provide outings for exercise and relaxation. Karen is prescribed powerful antipsychotic medication that must be closely monitored by a doctor. Laura talks to Jeanne weekly and travels to see Karen every other month. Karen's general health is good and her behavior and moods are currently stable. By necessity, her daily life is largely managed by others. Laura wishes and has dreams. She says, "If I could be closer to help her or find a group home or maybe a special working farm for young adults with special needs; I would feel relief." She asks, "What can I do to assure future care for Karen?" Laura receives postcards from her periodically. They are simple and written with a great deal of help from her social worker. Laura expresses her feelings, "I am thrilled to hear from her and simultaneously feel the loss, my grief, and the tragedy of her life."

A dream comes to her that describes her experience with Karen and the effect of chronic severe mental illness.

Dream: I'm in a dark building looking into another dark building at night, in a city of no particular size or shape. It may be a small town. The buildings are all low and not particularly close together. They're scattered about, not laid out with any plan, as they would be in a city. There are a few dim lights here and there, but none in the building across the way where I've been told Karen is. It's as if I am a visitor to this place. Someone is pointing out where Karen spends each night, awake. It is explained to me that this is the way she would and must have it. In total darkness.

After awhile I go outside and walk toward Karen's building. She comes out to greet me. She's dressed in dark clothes. She puts her arms around me. She tells me that she is sorry that she cannot work the way other people work, in the daytime, in the light, but that she does her work in total darkness. It's secret work, work that most people cannot see. The person who arranged my meeting with Karen has explained to me that this is so, that Karen does very important work at night, never missing a single one.

I know this and my heart aches to tell Karen that I know she toils at night, all night, and every night. I hold her and with my breath I press this thought into her. I want to tell her how brave and accomplished she is for the work she is doing. I want her to know that her life is admirable. I know that she knows that I love her. Before I can ask her about her work, she goes back across the open space between the two buildings, goes back to her work in the dark where she must be.

Never relieved of sorrow, Laura weeps quietly.

Two weeks pass. She has been visiting Karen.

Returning to analysis, Laura begins, "I have something really important to share." I hear urgency in her voice. Today she discusses her relationship with her younger son Mark. "This past week we spoke while I was traveling through New York City of my way back from seeing Karen on the West coast. Mark shared distressing news, telling me that 'something happened' while he was living and working in Germany several years ago." Laura has been suspecting that something has been bothering him for some time. She has suggested this occasionally to him and to me in analysis. For his own reasons, until now, he has been unable to talk with her and the family. He has withheld serious news from Laura for three years. In this recent conversation, Mark prefaces his news with a demand. Laura cannot share or reveal this to anyone else. In her new found strength she is *usually direct with him* insisting that she wants to know what's going on *and* that she must have support for herself, whatever the news. Laura presses him to let her speak with Eugene and her analyst. She stands her ground. He finally concedes and hands her a tiny photo of a beautiful three-year-old girl. In his brief explanation, he says that a woman, the child's mother, thinks this little girl is his child. Mark denies that he is the father is of this child.

Laura brings the photo to our face-to-face analytic session. The child has a lovely smile, brown hair, and bright eyes. When she shows the picture to me attempting to talk, her feelings pour out through anguished sobs revealing broken heartedness, elation, shame, hope, and aching confusion. She is sad and angry about her son's emotional withholding of such an important reality. "I would have helped in any way," she says. Laura tries in this session and subsequent sessions to understand what has gone so terribly wrong in her relationship with Mark. How could he keep his life so private, so separate from hers?

And yet, now, he is finally talking with her about his life and what he is dealing with as an adult. I ask what if she knows the child's name. "Sabina," says Laura through tears, "Sabina."

It's a heart breaking, shockingly painful exchange with her son, the tip of an iceberg: wondrous and cold. The hour is spent sobbing, a time of symbolically 'being on her knees'. I wonder about the complexities of Laura's first marriage, the early child raising years, and later, her single parenting, the effects of Karen's crisis and mental illness, and her former-husband's parenting. Secret keeping can be a learned behavior for guarding something, protecting someone, or some knowledge that is perceived as shameful or harmful. Secrets can also be about treasures, mysterious events, or things of value that are kept private for reasons we may never fully know.

Laura struggles in her analysis, over a number of sessions, to accept this complex reality. She finds a sense of wonder regarding this child amid the harsh and painful situation. In the tiny black and white photo Laura holds in her hands, she holds a living dream of a child who could be her granddaughter, one she cannot see or touch in the flesh. The paternity of the little girl is not clear; Laura must tolerate this unknown reality.

After this news and struggle to begin to integrate this complicated situation, both Laura and I remember and realize that the series of baby dreams she had reported during a three-year period was parallel to the birth and growth of this mysterious child. We had worked on the dreams concentrating on the symbolic baby, new life, and the "child" within Laura. The meaning of these dreams takes on additional dimension of depth now that Laura knows about the child's presence. Her dreams did reflect a birth within as she learns to care for herself and nurtures the "divine" child within her psyche.

Is it also possible that Laura's unconscious *knew* that a real baby had been born?

CHAPTER 15

Dreaming Fields of Gold and Turtles

Five years into Laura's analysis she has dreams of turtle visitations.

Since my move to Santa Fe months ago, my week long intensive Boston visit was reassuring to both of us. The telephone work was also settling into a pattern. This arrangement is effective and we maintain a trusting relationship, a secure attachment.

Dream fall during on my visit:

Visitations

Dream: There is a large field that I had been caring for – it's flat and golden with the new crop of whatever it is that has been planted. I go back and forth between my gardening/farming chores to a small structure where I take meals with others. Emma, my friend (we are adults in this dream) is there. She knows about my interest in turtles. I tell her I have seen a small one. One time, as I am leaving the communal eating place in the evening and heading toward the field where I sleep, I see an enormous turtle gliding over a ditch and up in an embankment, coming toward me. Emma says the turtle is looking for me, wants to see me, and has come to see me. I'm so happy to have its visit.

I think there must have been two visitations in the dream. The next time I see the turtle he's coming toward me in the field from another direction, again moving without the characteristic lumbering stride. It really does seem like gliding or floating in air. The turtle comes right up to me, much the way a dog might who was glad to see me. I'm on the ground as if camping out and ready to go to sleep for the night in the field, but there's still daylight. The turtle lands gently right beside me–half beside me and half on me–really cuddling as best a turtle can– with front legs around my shoulders and with his head in the curve of my neck. It's absolutely extraordinary. We are both so comfortable together like that. I can hardly believe the turtle has chosen to do this. I call out to Emma to bring a camera to record this event. "Don't worry," she says, "this is real." But every so often I pull my head back to get a good look at this marvelous creature. One reason I have doubts about this being a real turtle is its smoothness and its size. Its shell is about four feet long and rather narrow, and its head and neck and limbs are

beautiful and smoother to the touch than I would have imagined. The
face is so beautiful it reminds me of Henry (a young adult friend) and I
wonder if it isn't actually Henry playing a trick, just having some fun.
But the turtle just looks at me and cuddles up some more. He makes no
move to run away and seems content to stay a long while. All the same,
I call to Emma again to get the camera.

Laura's dream is set in the natural place she had most loved as a child and as an adolescent: the rural country boarding school. Emma was also a student there, and has been her dearest friend and confidant since fourth grade. In those years Laura felt at one with nature. She says, "I found a kind of heaven in nature as I tended and explored the earth." She planted and cared for the vegetable garden, which provided food that the students. They gathered vegetables and helped prepare the meals. They roamed the woods, waded in brooks, swam in rivers, nestled into grassy fields, and delighted in all kinds of creatures. The school's wheat fields were tended and harvested by local farmer. There she learned to care for and ride horses and camp on the land under the stars. She worked happily in the communal garden all summer. "I learned to be truly at home on the earth," she says with confidence, "and I learned about the importance of living in community. I didn't have much of a family and I didn't realize it then, but I learned to have deep, basic respectful connection with the earth, food, and interdependence of all life."

We continue to talk about the turtle in the dream. Laura suddenly remembers, "Recently, Gene and I were driving on the highway and approached a place where a large turtle had just been hit. It was crushed, bloodied, smeared across the road. I thought it must have been trying to cross the road, trying to reach or return to a stream nearby. It was an awful scene, the turtle slaughtered, blood all over, crushed shell and bones." Eugene pulled over and stopped the car just off the highway. She says she got out of the car with a blanket they carried in the trunk. "I gathered its smashed shell and soft guts with my hands putting this into the blanket. Eugene waved traffic around us. Laura says, "I carried the remains to a nearby field. Rubbed my hands in the grasses, then I was sick." She shivers and shakes her head as if trying to rid herself of the memory of the dead turtle and a feeling of nausea. I wait in quiet. She takes time to breathe and let the feelings in her body subside.

We agree that this dream is probably triggered by, or connected to the tragic road event and the depth in her feelings evoked by seeing and caring for the slaughtered creature.

Her dream is set in a field. She is very happy, joyful working with this dream. Laura has a quite a literal association as she really has spent a great deal of time in the fields both when young and now as an adult. In this dream she is responsible for her piece of earth, which *is golden with a new crop*. The dream suggests an intention of eventually nourishing the community. Laura's positive relationship with nature surrounds and supports her life. Nature is a form of the archetype of the "Good Mother" for Laura. This field is a symbolic space of the Great Mother and the symbolic place of Demeter, the Greek earth mother goddess. Demeter is associated with the earth, fields of golden grain, fertility, summer, and rhythms of organic growth. Laura knows that Native Americans once lived on this New England land; they are the ancestors of this place and especially the land of her school in her dream. She says, Native Americans call this land, North America, "Turtle Island." The dream says this is a *new crop*. I wonder to myself whether *new* growth is a renewed sense of nourishment from within her psyche, developing out of our therapeutic work, the 'nourishing crop' of a positive transference and counter-transference.

I reflect to Laura that this is the first dream reference to the color and light of *gold*. The appearance of such light is the opposite end of the spectrum from the darkness and opacity of her initial dream of the dark monolith, which she shared many years ago.

In the symbolism of alchemy, the appearance of gold refers to illuminated consciousness. Her capacity to experience life and light consciously is growing. Her depression was no longer in the foreground; she is now far more deeply engaged in relationships and life. Emma's move to New England is highly significant for Laura who truly cherishes her dear friend. They now spend time together frequently, talking, making art, and sitting in nature in the presence of the many local wild birds. With the early instability of Laura's parents and her very small nuclear family-life, the country boarding school community had been emotionally central to her since childhood. Emma shares this feeling and is Laura's "family" in so many ways.

This dream is set in the realm of the feminine, specifically Laura's personal feminine, which was occupied with collective work on and in the earth: farming, gardening, cooking, eating, and in relationships, particularly with women, nature, and animals. In this setting Laura was and is currently experiencing true happiness. She is emotionally open to the unexpected, not fearful, and she's quite expressive with Emma within the dream: familiarity, banter, joy, humor, and trust. Here, in this constellation of feminine emotional support and nourishment, Laura experiences a visitation by an ancient reptilian archetypal creature.

"I see a small turtle that is soon followed by another enormous four-foot-long turtle that floats and defies gravity. This is definitely not simply a familiar earth turtle," Laura says, smiling with pleasure. I then add, "It's a reptilian creature of earth and water that defies the rules and physics of daily, waking life. This turtle glides or floats upon the air. It is from an airy or etheric realm, the realm of spirits." Laura continues smiling at me. "Laura, why would this mysterious creature specifically seek you and why does it come now?" I ask. "I'm so interested in this creature, all creatures," she says after a moment of reflection, "perhaps it chooses me because I am not afraid." She pauses and her expression becomes somber, "And maybe in my gathering up the turtle's broken body on the highway and returning it to a place on the earth stirred something. Something resonated deep inside me." I wait to see if Laura will say more about the broken body. She doesn't.

We continue to explore the detail of the dream. After a bit of skepticism, she completely embraces the second visitation experience when the turtle comes gently to rest partly on her body. I pause and think for a moment, *this turtle is not acting like a reptile with an ancient brain; it is acting personally, with relatedness, such behavior would come with later central nervous system development, with evolution.*

I am moved by her dream and decide to offer a comment on biology. I don't give long explanations like this; yet, I felt moved. I venture, "This creature actually seems to be like us, an integration of ancient and modern evolution. We have a central nervous system with brain functions that operate unconsciously, such as breathing, heart function, and body temperature, and we have other brain functions that are conscious. The capacity for consciousness, the capacity for selective discrimination comes from activity in our forebrain that developed much later, after the reptiles and amphibians. I'm sharing this because your dream turtle is like the essence of dreams themselves." This seems to be a core moment in our work. Laura ponders and asks, "Can you say more?" I attempt to describe my understanding of the dreaming brain with my limits of vocabulary and understanding of the science of the brain and consciousness. "A brief and *very* limited description of my understanding, dreams may be an expression of the evolved mammalian brain. The reptilian brain, the most ancient part of our central nervous system, functions to regulate the deeper basic bodily functions such as breathing, swallowing, and heartbeat. Dreams are a functional expression of the evolved structures of the brain. The right and left hemispheres, other parts as well, orchestrate the processes of waking experience and those of the unconscious: sleeping and dreaming. Unconscious experiences and memories are complex constructions of stored information in the form of complex biological and electrical impulses, impulses organizing and forming images, sensation and sense memory, emotions, and bodily orientation. The brain with its hemispheres generally works in concert to discriminate order, body position in space, and understanding of images, languages, behavioral patterns, and emotions. If the mind is, in part, what the brain does, dreams are an expression of mind. Dreams expressing the collective unconscious have been shared in community as long as humans have lived. Artistic images expressed, even as early as 35,000 years ago in cave paintings in Lascaux, France, communicate stories and experiences. Structures and things were built for purposes and meaning- like the stones on a cord and the monolith in your initial dream. Oral stories were told for generations and written in pictures, petroglyphs and hieroglyphs, and later, letters that we still use. Dream work is making an unconscious brain process conscious. Greater discrimination of emotional experience, imagistic construction, and meaning can be translated into increasingly complex language, imagery, and understanding." Laura is listening carefully, following my comments. I know she has an inquiring mind with an active interest in the history of art, language, and science. From my experience I know that she will ask for clarification if she cannot understand. I add, "We are really just beginning to understand how the brain functions in human development, memory, emotional regulation, dreaming, ordinary and non-ordinary states of experience. It's a very exciting time in psychology and physiological biology. I cannot say what I know is totally accurate but I felt moved to go into this."

We move on to discuss what seems to be a similar pattern in a number of her dreams: she allows what seems *impossible* to exist and then she becomes *curious*. I find it unusual that within a number of dreams including this turtle dream, Laura wants to and actively records this mysterious visitation via photography. In her waking life photography is one of the arts she practices with a passion. "I want to bring the image back for others to see," she says enthusiastically. "On the one hand I am anxious to record, perhaps I won't be believed. If I take a picture, capture the image in the dream, when I return to be with other people in the dream, or when I wake up, I can verify the momentary experience for myself and share it with others. Maybe this is why I love photography. I can show others what I see, the *visions of my world*, my relationships." Laura's question, "Perhaps I won't be believed?" is a statement of her own self-doubt and skepticism. She is coming to terms with her own inner experience of creativity through dreams.

Animal visitation experiences in dreams have an aboriginal, shamanic quality. Laura muses, "My turtle creature is ancient and wise yet intimate and humorous. Normally a turtle is heavy; this one is as light as air. A flying turtle! I can be so heavyhearted, but I can be playful when I feel relief and safety. Maybe this creature really does express my wholeness. Maybe there is a divine comedy in life, maybe it's not all tragedy–something larger is at work after all."

The turtle's mysterious integration of opposites fascinates both Laura and me. The turtle, when it's neck is extended, has a phallic masculine appearance, reaching forward, asserting itself into the world. The round or oval body covered with a curved dome of bony shell or carapace suggests the feminine form, the eternal, that which is hidden within, and the circle. Turtles can withdraw into their shell and completely close the door to the outer world; this is total introversion and self-containment. The turtle as symbol is a carrier of the opposites of masculine and feminine, extroversion and introversion. Everything, wholeness, including what appear to be opposites, is contained within this one being. This creature represents the slow and steady pace of evolution that carries history, personal and universal, within and on the surface of its shell.

This dream and our long discussion have the effect of organizing and stimulating Laura's creative process. Still very much emotionally engaged and energized when she returns home; she begins to write poetry. This leads to other creative expressions: producing drawings and etchings, designing and planning to make a book by hand. This book will contain all these aspects under one cover. She decides to name this book, "Turtle".

Over the coming months, with the direction and support of her etching teacher and friend, Samuel, Laura chooses and sets old style metal type for the words. Laura and Samuel print her etchings and the pages of poetry on a large, very heavy, antique hand-driven press. With her familiar and thorough discrimination she chooses a fine, a moss-colored velum paper made of with suede-like material for the cover. She chooses delicate twined blue-green cords for closure strings. She assembles and binds ten copies by hand. Each book, printed with the title "TURTLE" in large gold letters is wound with its colored cord and is tied closed.

I listen closely to her creative process in our sessions. I make the observation, "The experience of making art has a similar quality to the turtle's arrival in your dream; it simply and mysteriously arrives. Laura you're open and curious, warmly receiving this visitor of creativity. You're ready and motivated. What a gift for you and for us that you can and do express your vision!"

Laura brings the poem she first wrote from the "visitation" dream that we worked on months ago. She had typeset and printed the poem on cream vellum paper.

TURTLE

In the darkness
and cold of a long
moonless night,
there comes a visitor
descending slowly,
legs outstretched
wavering upon the winter air.
Like a flat pebble
dropped upon the water
slicing from side to side
arriving gently,
belly to belly
with her host.

Turtle comes
with 13 shingles
on her oval roof.
Each one bears
two symbols
etched in green.
Through these
she sends her message
from the universe:
Lie still in times of pain.
Breathe deeply.
Do not run away.
Let each letter
come to you in
dreams from the night.

More and more, I see Laura consistently accepting opportunities to meet who and what arrives in her dreams *and* in daily life. I am not sure if she consciously knows that she is receiving instructions from deep within herself about how to be courageous and to deal with pain. I am sure she is receiving a subconscious message about coping.

During a snowy January night, a stray puppy finds its way into Laura's life. She tells the story, "I was alone at home and heard a crying animal, a very young animal. I went outside following the sound that was near the barn. I had a flashlight and found a shivering wet puppy crouched near the barn. It appeared so young, maybe two months old. I gathered it in my arms and brought the shaking puppy into the kitchen."

She describes tender care, first drying it with a towel, then wrapping it in a blanket, and sitting in the rocking chair by wood stove with the puppy in her lap. The puppy quiets, falls asleep. After a while Laura had created a nest of blankets by the stove, settled the sleeping puppy then called the local police. They have no alerts. Tomorrow she will call a vet and the county animal shelter.

After a week, no one has come forward to claim this little creature; Laura decides it's time for a companion for herself. Many years have passed since Laura had the time for or the pleasure of a puppy's companionship. The local vet pronounced the puppy healthy and gave it the proper vaccines. "This ball of yellow fur and sweetness appears to be, according to the vet, a Golden retriever mix. Laura decides to name this little female, "Turtle" after a recent series of dreams with visitations of turtles.

Laura offers herself to this new life and is satisfied playing with, walking, photographing and sleeping with her newfound companion. When Eugene arrives home from traveling, he too is delighted with the new family member of a loving golden puppy. Turtle is accepted as a gift from the universe.

CHAPTER 16

Meeting the Wise Old Woman Archetype

A dream of a benevolent old woman embodying the archetype of a wise woman arrives.

Here this ancient archetype is depicted as a helpful, wise, and mature woman. She represents feminine wisdom within each of us and is especially important within a woman. She is part of the Great Mother archetype in her benevolent form.

Dream: A long rain. The earth is unable to keep up with it. I am trying to get my family outfitted for the rain and the mud underfoot. I am walking on a dirt road and come to an old house that has used clothing and footwear–sort of an antique store. I look in the window and see all my old shoes and boots and those of my family in a corner of the darkened house. Some of the windows are broken and I climb inside and gather up as many pairs as I can carry: several of my old familiar shoes and boots and those of Karen. I take an armload back to where we are staying and then come back for Mark's boots. When I arrive at the old house, an old woman is there.

Laura stops reading and says, "She looks like an old potter I met in Paris years ago. She had a strange name, "Zingaro". I bought cobalt-blue plates, cups, and saucers from her."

Laura resumes:

The old woman gets the boots that I describe and hands them to me. I feel so much better having found protection for my family. This is an unusual antique store: the old woman just hands out the things that people need–like a relief center.

"I had this dream when Eugene and I were meeting with an attorney to do estate planning including updating our wills," Laura says. "We are finally able to save for a 'rainy day'. Gene's years of legal tangles and negotiations with his patents seem to be resolving." They are making plans for their future and the future for their adult children.

I say, " Laura there has been a *long rain* of grief in your analysis." She has been crying deeply in our sessions over the years, releasing long-repressed emotions, especially profound grief and trauma, stored over her lifetime. The deep sorrow can contribute to a muddy, soggy, heavy feeling in her body.

In this dream about the rain and boots, Laura boldly walks into an old house, *sort of an antique store*, through a broken window. She takes what she recognizes as hers. "Do you recognize the house?" I ask. I am wondering if this is a concrete memory or if it is a symbol representing a former, internal self-image. She does not currently live in this dream house; psychologically it is a part of her inner landscape. In this dream she is simply stopping there to collect things from her past experiences when her children were very young, in her first marriage. She sees shoes and boots belonging to her and her children. Together we notice that this is a darkened building and some windows are broken. The hardness of glass, which can be a description of psychological defensive barrier, in this dream it has shattered and that Laura is no longer separated from her feelings, no longer "outside of life looking in" and she steps in the building *without* permission and claims her things. "The place is not familiar, it's an antique store with old things, used clothing, and my personal things." Laura reflects. "But when I come back the second time an old woman is there and helps; she just hands out things that people need, well I mean, she hands me what I need." Laura is making the connection to her own past. We talk about this place, an old structure within her psyche that is largely deserted; it is her history, a storehouse of old things such as boots and used clothing that are protective and utilitarian. These boots provide a tougher "skin" useful for walking a path in the world through soaking rains. This is not a homey place; she can visit but doesn't need to live there. Yet there among these common, lost and discarded things there is a kind and generous old woman. She is the embodiment of humility.

Years ago, in her second analytic session with me, Laura had brought in a dream in which she described a pane of glass over a semi-abstract painting. We had discussed then that glass is a rigid transparent material that shatters under pressure or force. It serves to protect creative work and in that dream it acted as a mirror for Laura. *I can begin to see my reflection.* Now, in this later dream of a *sort of* antique store, there seems to be no separation between inside and outside. Some windows are shattered. She is *not* reflecting now; she is in life, in action and in charge of her energy. "I've had many roles and forms of work in my past. I wish my children could have protection and find their roles and purpose in their life journey."

We discuss what a "relief center" means; it is a place of assistance, help, and support. The purpose of such a center is to reduce a person's anxiety and "burdens" for a period of time. I remind her that it is a respite place, not a final destination. I sense that this is an analogy for our analytic, therapeutic, relationship. Relief is an emotional and physical release from anxiety. We are working together to return to her what is hers already, something she has lost or given away in the past. Laura has internalized a positive, humble, old woman helper and is finding the capacity for relief within. I point out to her that "relief" appears in the emergence of the archetype of a kind, wise old woman.

Laura shares more of her personal associations: "This dream reminds me of a trip to Paris many years ago where I met an old woman potter. She inspired me. As I think about it now, maybe she reminded me of Nonny, my beloved grandmother. I didn't realize that until now."

Laura pauses, and then says, "I recently visited the Holocaust Museum in Washington, D.C. The photographs, the structure of the exhibits, the architecture, everything was overwhelming. I felt horror in the room of shoes belonging to murdered men, women, and children. I know those shoes symbolized all the paths they had taken, all the lives lost, all the lives that had ended with such staggering malevolence. I sat in the archives reading stories for hours. I'm still trying to make sense of how this could have happened. I never met my paternal grandparents and German relatives, Christian Germans. What was my family's complicity? Did they know? What did they do? No one in my family ever discussed the Holocaust or their relation to it. Part of my family's complicity is the silence; we never talked about it. We never talked about so many, many things."

Laura's sense of helplessness in the face of the Holocaust Museum's awful truths and madness weighs heavily upon her heart, her soul. She is trying to find some meaning for the suffering in life. Now in her personal world, generosity and goodness can act to compensate for the horrors that exist. Perhaps the wise old woman appears in a dream precisely after the arousal of Laura's literally breathtaking, empathic response to contemplating the insanity, cruelty, and torture in the Holocaust during World War II.

We will sit together quietly for awhile, allowing feeling and bearing the horror and cruelty that is possible in mankind.

I express more of my thoughts on the dream to Laura, "A generous and compassionate woman offers relief, actually a kind of *re-living* from the wreckage of your past. She comes from within you. She is there to give back what is lost and what is needed for protection in the journey of life. She is a nurturing, generous feminine figure signaling a secure and repaired connection to the positive feminine in the unconscious."

Yes the wise old woman could be a compensatory figure *and* she is the other end of the spectrum of malevolent human behavior: humble helpfulness and goodness.

CHAPTER 17

Transitions and Sudden Loss

Six years have passed since we began this therapeutic work.

We have continued regular therapeutic work by phone and our seasonal Boston meetings. We've both taken time away from the treatment for various reasons. Among other things, these spaces of separation allow Laura to digest - to metabolize- the reintegration of her ego and personality to reflect a more mature understanding of her life. Much grief and rage that had been repressed and "split off" from consciousness has been experienced with a therapeutic witness and is released. Her life is more stable now and her mood is less depressed. She is taking a more active stance in her marriage, family relationships, philanthropic work, and her creative life. Laura's relationship with Emma is blossoming, both are happily engaged in their arts and enjoying the mutual emotional support that is especially dear in an old friend.

Difficult news reaches both Emma and Laura by letter. The alumni of their old boarding school have been notified that Alex has recently died in Germany. Laura calls me crying; "I just heard that Alex died suddenly of a heart attack. I'm stunned. It's unimaginable- him being absolutely gone. There's no way to say good-bye to this dear, dear man. I'm heartsick!" She is sobbing. There is no way now to bring closure to this incomplete, disrupted, significant relationship that was suspended in time and across space. Even though Alex and Laura did not see each other in later years, there was an understanding between them and, in that, a comfort. I am aware that *so many* profoundly important people in Laura's life have died suddenly, without warning, and without closure.

The boarding school successfully built a community that continues to function in place of an extended family. In her friendship with Laura, Emma, who also lost her classmate Alex, knows about Laura's tender, unrequited love for him. The women share a precious, supportive bond.

There is no cure for profound loss. Laura feels she cannot yet speak to Eugene about Alex's death. "I'm afraid to say anything. I can't let Gene know how much I still care for Alex. I don't want to hurt him." Laura speaks of this with sadness. She makes a decision not to share this pain; she is not yet ready to be open with her husband. This is her choice and a loss of another kind.

CHAPTER 18

Slowing Down

Spring of the seventh year of our relationship.

In our weekly analytic telephone session Laura describes a medical event two days ago that frightened her. Recently bitten by a tiny tick that caused a skin reaction, she went to the local hospital, carrying the offending insect in a tissue. The doctor examined her, studied the insect, and diagnosed Lyme disease, a deer-tick-borne illness. Laura was prescribed a powerful antibiotic. After returning home from the pharmacy she took the first dose. Home alone, she realized that she was having an unexpected severe allergic reaction to the medication: her legs began to swell and a rash appeared over her body. She was very frightened and immediately telephoned her closest neighbor who was able to take her back to the hospital. And because she'd only taken one dose her recovery was not complicated. The emergency room physician kept in contact. She was able to tolerate a different medication.

We discuss this frightening experience, "Scary but it all turned out alright," she says but goes on to talk about the reality of being home alone while Eugene travels for his work. She is feeling especially vulnerable tonight and we take this opportunity to address her general health. "I'm slowing down physically," she tells me, "and doing less traveling." It is nearing the time of her yearly blood work that includes reviewing liver enzymes levels. With her history of hepatitis B and C certain blood and liver enzymes elevate when the virus is activated. The surprise allergic reaction has broken through her psychological defenses. The upcoming blood tests are triggering her anxiety. Usually she is able to keep her vulnerability out of awareness, in the background, out of consciousness.

She then reports a dream of an older wise woman, the second appearance of this archetypal figure. In this encounter the older woman has a personal gift for Laura and a mysterious dark young man appears.

Dream: I am introduced to a dark young man in a dark city. I feel deeply connected to him the moment we meet. We have to travel somewhere.

We have our arms resting on the back of a chair with coats on it. His hand rests lightly on my shoulder and my hand gently holds the fabric of his shirtsleeve. He is beautiful with dark soft curls all around his head. His smile is calm and radiant. We are happy together. I don't know where he came from.

As we sit there feeling so close, yet not sitting exactly side by side, I look down at his hand on my shoulder and am surprised to see that it is black. He is being called away somewhere and I know that this time together is limited and about to end. I feel his arm; it's terribly boney. It's the feel of a man who has been starved and deprived; yet his hands and face are beautiful and healthy looking.

The moment comes when we have to stand and go our separate ways. There are plenty of acquaintances to go with me, but I see no one for the young man. Despite this, he moves confidently into the crowd of people. I head back to the apartment where I am staying with my husband. It's a place we have borrowed for the night and there is only one key between us. Gene and I have gone our separate ways for the day. I am walking with newly made friends toward the apartment at night, realizing I don't have the key and don't remember where the apartment is exactly. We all keep walking anyway and come to a street crossing where the traffic has been held up for some reason.

I look up and see that the young man has flagged down a convoy of bicycles that travel and serve some purpose in the city. He leaps easily on a bicycle while it's moving and barely pauses long enough to let an elderly woman hop onto the handlebars in front of him. Perhaps it is his mother? She has his same short curly hair.

The old woman sees that I am crying and holds up a beautiful silk shirt the color of red bricks. She motions to me to catch the shirt so I can wipe away my tears. She lets the shirt go and the wind carries it right to me over the crowd. A younger woman nearby says to me, "Oh, you will have a wonderful, rich compost. Take all the cloths you use to dry your tears and put them in the compost. That's what we do here."

"He was like a young Greek god," Laura muses.

"You meet in a dark city," I say. "He could be a fellow traveler or maybe a guide? Your dream says *we have to travel somewhere.* You have a brief time together in physically tender awareness, as if in a waiting room or station." We discuss the dream figure of the dark young man who is called to go and has to go alone. My intuition is stirred when Laura mentions a Greek god and I ask, "Might he be related to an ancient Greek god, Hades? or even Hermes, who also known as Mercury."

I pause, "Hades, Pluto is his Roman name, is a male divinity, mysterious, and unknown, although the man in your dream is younger and less powerful than the mythic Hades, lord of the underworld." Hades/Pluto represents the archetypal energy of death and rebirth. It isn't clear what divinity this dream figure may be associated with- we use these descriptions to open up associating to the dream's meaning.

Within Laura's dream he appears as an inner masculine figure, an aspect of the archetype of the *animus*. The *animus* could take many forms; here he has a beautiful youthful masculine presence leading away. Jung referred to the *animus* as contra-sexual (opposite gender) figures within a woman's unconscious psyche. For a man his contra sexual figures, his inner feminine, is described as the *anima.*

Laura and the mysterious man establish a brief and intense relationship, a deep and erotically charged bond. When the dark man leaves her, Laura tries to find, to return to, or have a reunion with, her husband. They are sharing a borrowed apartment. She cannot remember where the apartment is. She cannot find the key. The dream is saying that the marital space is temporary, she cannot go home, she cannot return to the familiar, secure place. She doesn't know how to find her husband. She experiences anxiety and sadness about being lost and separated from her husband.

We discuss the appearance of a dark man who is also described as black. We both remember and discuss that several years ago she dreamed of a group of African American black men. In the dream she felt horror and helplessness as she witnessed their lynching. At that time we discussed the oppression of racism, human cruelty, and the history of slavery. We talked about what was oppressed in her. What is strangled, lynched? Who is the strangler within herself? Is there something she is killing?

We return to her dream; this man is different. The singular dark and black young man in this dream is free, *calm and radiant,* yet his body seems deprived, starved. "This man is nearly beatific," Laura says, "and later, he is joined by a loving figure, I think she is his mother. He is not traveling alone after all." Within the dream there is an instant of realization for Laura, the words in the dream are so clear and powerful, *the moment comes when we must each stand and go our separate ways.* She notes this aloud but does not dwell on this realization, nor does she seek its meaning now. We speak about the apartment in the dream as a transitional space, a place where she and her husband have been staying. She explains to me that this is actually a regular practice for them when traveling for business meetings. In this dream, Eugene and Laura share "one key," perhaps this is the marriage itself, their relationship, and in some ways they lead separate lives. She feels distressed in the dream when she has trouble finding her way back to the apartment. Laura begins to share these feelings, "I do feel as if Eugene and I have gone our separate ways so often, especially on business trips, but also many times in our lives. We always seem to find our way back to each other." I feel that Laura is describing her reality honestly.

"In the dream I feel the young black man is the kind old woman's son," Laura says. "Do you think she is the wise old woman? Do you think she is the archetype of the wise old woman who appeared in my dream some time ago?" Laura remembers the woman in that dream who was at the relief center returning her boots in the rain. I say: "In that dream, the old woman was recognizing your feelings of need and she responded with returning your own things."

"In this dream encounter," Laura rereads from her dream notebook, *The old woman sees me crying and holds up a beautiful silk shirt the color of red brick. She motions to me to catch the shirt so I can wipe away my tears. She lets the shirt go and the wind carries it right to me over the crowd.*" I see that in this moment Laura is beginning to experience the meaning of "gift"; she is beginning to understand that the psyche is granting, or endowing her with a specific gift. The wind, spirit itself, carries the gift, like in her turtle visitation dreams before, the gift is meant to go directly to her, over the crowd, over the collective of whom she is a part. The gift is sent from a compassionate and wise mother archetype, a gift straight from the unconscious. The wind or the element of air is sometimes called *pneuma*, as in "pneumonia," and represents the presence of the spirit in dreams. Laura now recognizes that the red silk shirt is a divine gift of the psyche. I know that the color red, and especially red silk, is associated with rich meanings for her. Red is a color representing the essence of life, lifeblood, and bloodlines in families.

During her analysis Laura has done research on her maternal ancestors, great-grandparents. It was quite exciting for her to find that they started a silk business in New England. They imported silk worms, had a factory for spinning the silk, and employed many factory workers to weave the cloth. Laura's early interest in textiles and weaving appears to be "in her blood".

The color red, and red silk, have appeared in her dream before her analysis began: the triumph of the eagle, with red blood appearing from its wounds. In a later dream in analysis, after the completion of her art studio, which was a momentous achievement in her life:

two red birds fly in a ballet, carrying a red silk banner as they arrive in my studio.

At the end of this recent dream an additional feminine presence; a *younger woman nearby* instructs her: *Oh, you will have wonderful, rich compost. Take all the cloths you use to dry your tears and put them in the compost…*

"Perhaps this is your 'internalized analyst's voice' encouraging you," I say to Laura. The message here is to realize there is a way to transform grief, to bring new life out of past suffering. Laura is birthing, growing, her inner advisors and helpers. The red silk shirt both absorbs her tears and can become compost. There is salt residue in tears. Salt is an elemental substance, an essential substance needed for life. Our lives are made of the threads of experiences woven in an organized way, all contributing to the 'cloth' of our life.

I think about stories and myths from around the world and across time that tell us: the salty tears of sorrow are the necessary ingredients for the realization of wisdom. Laura, who is a gardener, knows "compost" is the language of organic change. It is the natural cycle of life and death. She understands that compost is the basis for new life, renewal. She is realizing that her sorrow can contribute something else, unseen at this point.

Laura says, "I'm feeling, reassurance, kindness, and guidance in this dream."

I feel that the final line of the dream, *"that's what we do here,"* describes the process of Jungian analysis and dream work. We use the wisdom that can be found in suffering and through working with and honoring the unconscious. We raise it to consciousness. Wisdom requires bearing tension, experiencing difficult feelings, metabolizing meanings, and integrating this into the personality and everyday life. This goes on over and over again. This process supports the renewal of life.

The literal regeneration or renewal of life, however, is not manifesting in physical form for Laura. Her body's health is declining.

CHAPTER 19

Confrontation With the Shadow

It's midsummer of the summer seventh year of analysis.

Laura receives a call informing her that her ex-husband, the father of her sons, has suddenly died of a massive heart attack in California. On the phone with me she is distraught. She cries, wails, "They have no idea. The pain of my children's loss is hardly bearable; they have no idea yet. I ache for them, for me. I've lost so many people, all so suddenly. It's the end of my hope that he will really be in their lives in a helpful way."

Within a month of this shattering news, Laura reads me her dream of a baby, the fifth and final of the baby series, over seven years.

Dream: I enter a large square room painted white. It is empty except for a high hospital bed. A woman lies curved within white sheets on the bed. There is a trembling air of expectancy. I have entered the room at that terrible moment just before disaster strikes. A baby cries. The woman is lying on her right side with her back to me. I see her raise her left hand high beneath the sheet. The baby shrieks now. The woman is about to crush it with one blow from her extended hand that's pulled back to gather its full force.

From across the room, I open my mouth to scream and my voice pierces everything, drowning out the crying of the baby. My voice rings throughout the room and stays the woman's hand in mid-air. Slowly she lowers her arm to her side. It lies limply over her hip. I move toward the bed slowly, silently, or as if approaching a wild animal. The woman turns her head toward me and the sheet that covers her and the baby falls away from her face. I am not prepared for what I see. Her nose is swollen double its normal size and is red as a child's ball. Her right cheek is purple like raw hamburger meat. My heart leaps toward her as if bursting out of my chest. I kneel beside the bedside half in prayer, half to be able to touch her left leg that hangs over the near edge of the bed. A male hospital attendant comes into the room. I ask the woman if I may put my hands on her leg. She answers "yes" and I put my palms on her, one on her knee and one on her shin. She tells me my hands are

*cool and feel good on her hot skin. She begs the attendant to bring her
clean sheets. Then she gets up and takes the baby into the bathroom. As
the bedding is peeled away I see it is soaked in urine from top to bottom.
I look at the bed, this terrible bed, with its grid of rusted springs hooked
end to end, the foundation for mortal violence, and watch as pristine
white sheets are smoothed over it. I feel utterly drained. I climb onto
the bed and lie there stretched out, warming the cool bedding until the
newly returning mother and baby arrive.*

The dream is stunning. We are speechless.

After minutes in mutual silence, Laura finally says: "A brutalized,
raging mother comes close to murdering her baby. Who is this? My
god, is this really me?" We sit quietly. Laura is realizing her deeply
buried explosive rage is taking a form and it is difficult to bear. It's
awful to face one's rage and one's capacity to do harm, to be vicious.

This dream is, or seems to be, evoked by many things, including
the recent sudden loss of her first husband, the father of her two children. Memories from the best of times to the most awful times flood
into her mind with news of his death. Nick wouldn't allow the very
young children to see their mother when she was hospitalized weeks
for breast cancer. His death is yet another, shocking profound loss.
This is the sixth death in a series of deeply personal and traumatic losses. With the exception of her grandmother, Laura's loved ones all died
suddenly. Laura's miscarriage of her first pregnancy at five months,
her mother, her father, Alex, and now Nick; all the adults died of heart
attacks. She is overwhelmed with feelings.

This dream seems to be a convergence of all the pain and torture
that Laura feels in her body and mind, the horror of her many personal
tragedies, and the horror of our human capacity to murder.

From Laura's earlier experiences, she had come to perceive hospitals as places of torture and isolation; now, in this dream, a hospital
can also be found to be a place for rest and healing. This dream signals
the pinnacle of her rage against the tragic horrors in life, especially in
her own life. Simultaneously she finds the courage to express mercy
and compassion.

This is Laura's epiphany, her moment of realizing self-compas-
sion for her life. Laura is confronting her personal, and the collective,
shadow.

This is her ego's confrontation with rejected, denied, and repressed aspects of herself. These are intolerable, nearly unbearable,
inner experiences that may be based in her body memory and emotional experience as well as the collective unconscious. If Laura is to
be authentic, integrated, and approaching wholeness, she must see the

dark side of her Self. In the terminology of Jung's analytic psychology, this is the confrontation with the *shadow*. The greatest shadow of life is death. Although she is not consciously stating this, I feel, intuit, that this dream is the beginning of facing her own death, her impending physical annihilation. We know this reality is in the background of her consciousness, not in focus now. In this dream she is revealing the mad, wounded, exhausted woman within, the raging, suffering, murderous mother. She is confronting the dark side of the Self, the archetype of the Terrible Mother, the destructive part of the Great Mother. This dream contains the enormous tension of the dark and light forces within each of us. Finally she has the capacity, the ego strength, to act, to scream with her entire being, and stop the murder.

With her health and energy waning, she won't have the strength to use her psychological defense of the *denial* of her coming death. Laura shows great courage and trust in me, in our relationship, to share this glimpse of the murderous mother within. I know, from my own experience in childhood and my experiences of motherhood, that the exhaustion and depletion of physical and emotional reserves can shred one's capacity to love and to care continuously, tenderly, and unselfishly for one's infant or child. Laura trusts me as an analyst and as an experienced mother. This is a dark and difficult place within each woman that is so hard to face. Yet, it is easier to face our flawed capacity by way of a dream than in waking daily life. Laura's dream reflects the socially unacceptable, hidden experience of being tired, deprived, and drained of the life energy needed for personal survival, let alone to care for a hungry, frightened, needy baby. Throughout her life Laura has suppressed and sublimated her exhaustion and frustrations in many ways.

I think about Laura's powerful dream and reflect to myself that the mothers I have treated over years of my work do act out their anger, but as far as I knew, none to such violent extremes. The women I have worked with have been able to find family, friends, and/or professional help for their rage, angst, and depression. I know mothers who share or confess, much later in their lives, behavior and thoughts they were ashamed of, ways they were mean, limited, and selfish. I have worked with women who bear the physical and deep emotional scars of the hatred, violence, and cruelty of their own mothers. If they have a choice, they often choose not to bear children, partly in fear of repeating their mother's horrific behavior.

When we learn of a parent's acting out that takes the form of injuring or killing an infant or child, we feel shock and horror. For those of us who are parents, somewhere deep within, we are each relieved that this was "not me." Here I am speaking of *mother* referring to the primary caregiver. Mental illness, perversity, terrorization, and evil exist in spite of our denial and our wish that these horrors didn't exist.

In the human collective unconscious, across cultures and time, there is an archetype of a terrible, negative mother. Her extreme form exists within each of us, though generally deeply buried in the unconscious. She is known by many names: "witch", Kali the destroyer of Hindu tradition, and the Gorgon of Greek mythology. Her horrific gaze, her evil eyes, can turn one to stone. As mothers, as humans, we need to know our capacity for aggression, negativity, and our *dark* energy lest we project this archetype on to other women and men nearby and far away.

Knowing Laura intimately, I surmise that she did suffer as an infant from her parents' effort to "correct" her immune system by allowing their physician to administer poorly understood radiation procedures. In her childhood it is unclear why Laura was allowed to suffer from inadequate anesthesia during two surgeries. Laura experienced abandonment during her mother's "nervous breakdown" and depression when she was three-years-old. It's possible her mother struck her more then she remembers when she was a young child. There was a lack of adequate emotional support from both of her parents throughout her adolescence and early twenties. There were failures and a pattern of neglect, often with unintended ignorance, by her personal mother, especially regarding the lack of protection of her bodily integrity. Laura miscarried her first pregnancy at five months with no one there to help her. Her mother died before that pregnancy and wasn't there for her later pregnancies. Laura felt abandoned. She wished that her mother had been there to celebrate the initial news of her first pregnancy and wished that her mother had been there to help her bear that loss then and, later, the joys of her two children's lives. Abuses of commission-actual violence in one form or another and abuse omission-neglect both occurred. It is quite possible that she too neglected her children. It is important to remember that even with the darkness of neglect and abuse parent(s) may also be loving and generous at times.

Laura bore the hospital's error in giving her unscreened, disease-infected blood. It was not intentional although the medical establishment did fail her. From my perspective, Laura felt the deadly hand of the archetypal negative terrible mother with her breast cancer and treatment, followed by the cruel, ill-fated hepatitis diseases carried in surgical blood transfusion. She bore her older daughter's mental illness without the support of her former husband. In Laura's unconscious, the archetype of the negative, or the terrible mother was activated. She was experiencing the archetypal, biblical trials of Job. She struggled with her "angels," and raged at the unfairness of it all. Laura wondered aloud for herself, and for all those murdered in colonialism, slavery, war and holocausts, "How could God allow this?"

When we do the long, hard work of owning our shadow complex: the shameful, disgusting, unacceptable, and disregarded aspects ourselves; we no longer need to identify with, or become possessed by, or merge with the shadow complex. The shadow complex, with its deepest root in the unconscious, is in human experience. The deepest root of the human shadow is evil, destruction, and perversion of innocence. And, we generally feel that the opposite of life is death. Our psychological work is to become conscious, to make choices as consciously as possible from a place of compassionate relatedness, and to be willing to repair what we damage, including damage to ourselves.

In the dream Laura and I are witnessing the ugliness and horror of brutality. We see impending infanticide in its most extreme form, a mother potentially killing her baby with her own hand. The tension in the dream is palpable to Laura and to me. Will the mother kill the infant or not? Will she destroy the needy, less-developed part of herself, her potential creativity and futurity?

This is a nightmare with stark presentation of the opposites of good and evil set in a large square room painted white. The room is an earthly place with a hospital bed. Laura knows it should be a place of treating what is most sick, the place of healing. But this has not been her personal experience. Laura must face, approach, and touch this horror and attempt to soothe the monstrousness of her own murderess madness in the face of bodily horror, brutality, illness, and dis-integration shown by this woman figure. She must bear her own fear of approaching a scene of possible murder, her own injury, or death. She risks annihilation by getting too close to the mad woman who could just as easily turn on her.

In the dream, Laura releases a piercing scream, giving voice to her horror. Her voice is a pure, primitive, mammalian sound of alarm. That sound has the power to stay the woman's hand in mid-air, unlike Laura's screams in childhood operations with too little anesthesia. Now, she hears her own scream and stops the violence. Laura hears her own piercing cry of alarm. She fearfully approaches the wounded, crazed woman. Laura is trembling with fear *and* simultaneously feeling compassion. She bears the enormous tension of the opposites; for this capacity we must have a strengthened ego complex formed via deep human attachment, "a secure base" and we must do hard work of psychological maturation. When such terrible experiences occur and we are too young or underdeveloped, our ego and personality become overwhelmed, our senses are flooded, confused, chaotic, understanding and integration become impossible, we shatter, we dissociate. We feel and may describe our experience, "I feel broken. I was broken." Unbearable experiences are held in the unconscious, and are *un-experienced*. We need the presence of a safe human being to consciously experience and attempt to integrate the "unbearable".

This is an awe-filled, tremendous experience of the dark side of the Self. In this dream Laura's ego is *not* identified with *murderousness*. Her ego is identified with compassion in action ... *my heart leaps toward her as if bursting out of my chest*.... Laura's courage in attempting to stop the deadly *crushing* blow changes the course of repeated generations of violence. Laura's act is an act of redemption of the rejected, shameful, damaged mother and wounded woman. This is Laura redeeming the wounded, murderous mother within herself. This is an act of Self-redemption.

Laura has never before mentioned during our sessions together the use of prayer to cope with her fears. In the dream, Laura *kneels beside the mad, exhausted mother, half in prayer*. *Half* is not full surrender to the divine, *half* in order to gently touch the woman. Reaching out and touching is a profound human gesture. Laura moves to save the baby, a vulnerable new life. In reaching out to touch and make physical contact, Laura preserves the basis of survival: human relationship. In the dream, Laura is the dream "ego" or personal self consciousness that we identify with; she offers humane contact to a distraught woman, the archetypal negative mother, who has been in shadow deep within Laura's unconscious: a woman who has been brutalized and left in her own stinking mess. Laura, as the dream-ego, is fully engaged in an act of compassion. At the deepest level this is an act of Self-healing. Significantly, the psychic and physical tension is held in Laura's scream and the mother's "stay of hand." The murderous impulse is transformed by her act of loving-kindness. The new life, the baby is saved.

Collectively, women and mothers, including the planet *mother earth*, are suffering and have been devalued in many cultures. Laura has to *literally* touch and smell the woman's raw body. She must feel and sense the experience of desperation and putrid waste. This dream shows a stark contrast to Laura's normal personality presentation, or persona, of a sweet, clean, lovely, healthy, and well-organized woman. This is the moment of Laura choosing *not* to abandon her deepest, most wounded feminine Self.

The shadow's ugliness, horror, madness, and despicable state cannot be denied in the pursuit of wholeness. In the dream, Laura chooses to approach the horror, to bear her fear and trembling, and to trust something greater, though unnamed. *Mortal violence has occurred here.*

I wonder to myself if Laura, in this dream, is unconsciously remembering and repairing her miscarriage in the fifth month of her first pregnancy. Years ago she shared, "It was a bloody event in a bathroom and later in the hospital with feeling, being, totally out of control." She could be remembering and repairing the experience of loss of her own mother during very early childhood, when her mother was hospitalized with a "breakdown." Not all historic events are consciously recalled within a session, yet the impact of such a powerful dream gives access to the *emotional core* in past experiences. Laura is releasing repressed agony and horror, giving voice and birth to her pain in the presence of herself. She is witnessing herself in the presence of a witnessing other-her analyst.

In the dream, after this confrontation, an unknown silent male attendant, a humble helper, enters the room. Laura says, "The wounded, soiled woman is begging for his help." He hears her and silently responds to her plea to bring *clean sheets*. I reflect on this and say, "He responds to her needs, affirming her and brings a form of comfort and protection." I suggest that in this dream the attendant is an active animus capacity within her. He is a humble servant: attending, listening, and providing what is required, needed. We have these parts within ourselves, our helpers.

Toward the end of the dream, the woman and her baby disappear into the bathroom. Laura describes her associations to bathroom: "A very, very private room for change: purification of my body, immersion in water, and letting go of bodily wastes. It's a place I can see my body, my scars. I prefer to be alone in the bathroom. It is a place of refuge for me."

At the dream's conclusion, Laura *climbs up into the bed, and lies there stretched out, until the newly returning mother and baby arrive.* Laura rests in the bed on cool, clean sheets. I say, "In essence Laura the bed is now becoming a shared 'psychological' space for you, the mother, and the baby; you are becoming integrated."

Confrontation with her shadow is *exhausting psychological work.* Her childhood nightmare fear of *disembodiment and bodily disintegration* do not manifest here. She bears the enormous tension without shattering. Toward the end of the dream Laura says, "*I feel utterly drained.*"

CHAPTER 20

Worms

It's late summer of the seventh year of analysis.

Dream: I have a worm infestation. I pull long, thin worms out of my belly.

September.

It is now early autumn and I am in Boston for our seasonal week of face-to-face sessions.

Not long after our work with the dream of confronting her negative mother complex, signs of resurgence in Laura's liver-related illness begin to appear in brief, disturbing dreams. I am glad to see her in person as she's facing health issues. She recently returned from her wilderness retreat in Canada. Today she's wearing a sleeveless shirt that fully reveals her arms. Her skin is slightly puffy and somewhat pale. Unusual I think, especially after a several weeks spent in nature. I do not comment on her appearance at this time.

We talk about the worm dream. These worms, primitive creatures, come from within, an *infestation* in her gut, her belly. The worms are emerging into consciousness and she is making physical contact., attempting to pull them out of her body. An *infestation* generally implies *many*, a negative, unwanted appearance of some creature which threatens bringing disease. When she reports this dream I wonder if perhaps she is feeling that she is *"handling it"*? Laura is not expressing horror or even mild revulsion. I feel it. I wonder to myself if am I experiencing her unutterable feelings? Her denied feelings may be unconsciously, automatically *split off*, or repressed, or experienced by the analyst. It is also true that I do have my own reactions to this dream and I am worried about what this may mean. Psyche and soma are unified. I find this an odd, disturbing dream of primitive, non-vertebrate creatures infesting her body. These creatures are feasting upon her life energy, multiplying deep inside her body cavity. They are invading Laura's gut and she is pulling them out through her flesh. In her discussion of the dream she says, "I urgently want them out!"

She raises the possibility of an actual parasitic infestation. She wonders aloud if perhaps this is a concrete problem with a solution, "Did I contract a parasitic infection from the water while we were traveling? We traveled to a tropical place this past spring, stayed on an island." She promises me that she will immediately arrange medical tests with a laboratory that specializes in illness caused by parasites. I think that Laura is making this into a concrete problem with a real solution. It would be more convenient, less worrisome, and it also could be a form of psychological defense, denial.

Later in the week, in another session, Laura reports another dream.

Dream: A squirrel attacks me. I cannot shake off its bite. Its teeth are sunk into my ankle.

I note to myself that this second invasion or penetration by another life form. A small mammal makes this incursion; this creature approaches her from outside of her body. Laura associates: "The squirrel reminds me of the nagging demands of life." I ask about this small mammal's oral aggression toward her and I'm aware that squirrels *are not* carnivores. This dream squirrel was not trapped or cornered; under those circumstances one could expect aggression, a normal reaction in a wild mammal. I'm wondering if this squirrel is rabid?

Laura says, "I don't have the energy anymore to keep up with the demands on me, those make on myself and by others, my husband, children, extended family, and friends, care of the house and garden. I feel the weight of it all and am irritated with everyday tasks." She reflects on "squirrely," behavior. I ask, "What's grabbing onto your ankle, holding you back, causing you pain and injury? What is 'squirrely' in you?" She then focuses on the specific demands of various family members. We aren't looking at the possibility of the squirrel being infected with rabies, similar to the worms infesting her in the last dream. *What is "squirrely" in Laura that she cannot yet, or will not, explore in analysis?*

An animal or instinctual energy that is normally perceived as natural and industrious, in this case, a squirrel, is appearing in Laura's dream as dangerous: *its teeth are sunk into my ankle.* An aggressive psychological *complex* of feelings, or something else, will not let go, cannot let her rest. It could infect her, is frightening her, and it is surely slowing her down.

Two dreams this similar and in such close appearance are alarming, they're supposed to be alarming. They are warning dreams. She is attempting to rid herself of these problems, to shake them off, to minimize the intrusive disturbances. She isn't succeeding. There are no helpers in these dreams. She is distressed and in denial, pushing the thoughts away. Laura's life-long benevolent relationship with Mother Nature is shaken with dreams such as these.

Physical symptoms help us to become aware of deeper organic processes. Our psyche-soma, or body-mind, is integrated. A highly complex organism, we usually are NOT conscious of what is going on inside our organ systems. The physical body knows organic realities, such as illness or pregnancy, well before our conscious mind can acknowledge or assimilate such signals and realities into conscious language and meaning. From experience, I know that physical illness can sometimes be signaled in dreams. Listening to her dreams and feeling my own discomfort with the images raises red flags for me. Laura is reporting feeling unable to keep up with the daily life demands. This is the first time in seven years that Laura expresses feeling real physical limitation. It's the first time I have ever seen her appearing to be ill. Alarmed, I share my observations with her, urging her to seek medical evaluation. She says she will.

I fly home after my week in Boston and follow up by telephone regarding her health. She had arranged an immediate appointment with her internist after our discussion. She reports continuing listlessness and increasing debilitating fatigue. Her doctor appointment was yesterday. She reports that her internist, a man she likes and trusts performed a physical exam and sent her for extensive blood tests. She is waiting for the results.

PART-II

The Journey of Dying and Death

CHAPTER 21

Terminal Diagnosis

Early October, the seventh year of analysis.

The blood tests confirm that her liver enzymes are soaring. Her internist meets with her: "Highly elevated liver enzymes Laura; we knew this could happen." After another examination and deep palpitation of her belly, he expresses urgent concern that there is a growth, probably a tumor, in her liver. This shocking news marks the beginning of Laura's accelerated search for specialists and consultants. She calls friends who know friends who can help make referrals if needed.

Laura has resisted this tidal wave of awareness for years; preferring to row her boat, take her chances, with the calmer, sweeter waters of alternative medicine. Over the last few years she studied the Indian medicine and heath practices of Ayurveda and began cooking a diet with natural ingredients and using herbs from India. Such actions comforted her and the food agreed with her physiology. "I am more clear-minded," she says. She had stopped the use of even the smallest amount of alcohol, chocolate, and most sugar. She spent time in nature gardening and walking daily.

With all these efforts Laura could not prevent the blossoming of liver cancer, which developed from the hepatitis C viral infection contracted fatefully thirty-six years ago. Laura's life was full and vibrant; the quality of her life had been very good until recently. I would like to think that the disease has been suppressed longer due to her proactive efforts in self-care.

After a brief telephone conversation with a well-known and respected Boston Internist a specialist Liver, Hepatic disease, Laura is able to secure an immediate referral to Massachusetts General Hospital's team of hepatic oncology specialists. Her battery of tests, many will be painfully invasive, is scheduled.

It's now the end of October of the seventh year of the analysis. We are in touch regularly by telephone; it's been a over a month since we last met face-to-face in Boston. Laura and Eugene make the drive into

Boston for their quickly scheduled Mass. General appointments. She calls me at my home and leaves a telephone message with this information. When I receive her message I can hear a hitch in her breathing as she informs me of the discomfort and difficulty that she has begun to experience while trying to take deep breaths. She says, "I'll call you from home in a day or two, after the specialists review my tests and examine me."

Three days pass.

Finally Laura calls to share her experiences. Her voice is not strong although her mood is cheerful. "Imagine, me sitting in a waiting room at Mass. General, the Mecca of western medicine. I don't really want to be in any hospital. For thirty-six years I've carried the seeds of this potential death sentence. It's such a paradox. I received life-giving blood from a hospital never suspecting this might lead to cancer."

Silence.

No longer cheerful, she says, "The bad news is that my body can no longer suppress the virus." The liver tumor had been quietly mushrooming and had entwined itself around her hepatic aorta with barely a symptom until the fatigue, increasingly serious fatigue.

Symbolically speaking, the dark river Styx, which touches the shore of death in the Greek underworld, is opening before her. The current of bad news is swiftly flowing.

Laura describes sitting in the waiting room for a very long time. The room was filled with very ill patients prior to the meeting with a team of specialists. "I felt like I was with other pilgrims; we're hoping for healing. We all want our lives saved. We came to drink the waters, hoping for a cure here at Mass. General, a secular Lourdes." I remember that Lourdes is a French shrine where miracles are said to occur. Pilgrims come from around the world to drink the waters. Laura continues, "Sitting there, I felt a strange, silent fellowship. I'm sure we were each preoccupied with our own stories and degrees of illness."

She tells me that, during the wait, "Gene, who is never able to sit and wait for long, paced then asked if he could go look up something; he went off to find the medical library, medical students, and the bookstore, anything or anyone who might shed light on this illness and prognosis." She says, "After awhile he returned with a bag of books and a plan."

As she speaks to me on the phone about her experience at Mass. General I feel sadness. My mind races while trying to cope with my realizations as I hear her words and labored breathing. Would a *darshan*, a holy meeting and blessing from a guru in India, or a ceremony with a Native American shaman, be of help? I think of seeing Laura and

Eugene sitting with others in a Mass. General hospital waiting room and in my imagination that room transforms into a life raft. It's swaying under the emotional weight of the very, very ill people in these very rough waters. And now, from a distance, I picture this little raft taking on water, slowly sinking, each passenger flailing or floating into the sea of ultimate change.

I pray for a better outcome for this terribly serious illness. Coming back to the present moment I listen to Laura, "Eugene always moves into his finest genius when a challenge arises. He works well, thrives, under extreme pressure. Ironically, *he's* the one who's collapsed with health crises- high blood pressure and exhaustion- after the completion of every enormous project. I'm thinking about sitting at his bedside in different hospitals across the country, fearing his death and waiting for his return from utter exhaustion. I find it so strange that I'm the ill one, now that we're just on the edge of retirement."

Laura describes her feeling at seeing Eugene's return to the waiting room. "I was so happy to see him, felt lifted by his enthusiasm. I love him, his hope. He said wants to create a tool and method. He wants to save me." Listening to her, I think to myself that I am sure his research and enthusiasm barely cover the edge of his agitated anxiety in this situation. His creative scientific inquiry and devoted hard work are his ways of caring and mobilizing in the face of a huge wall of unknowns and darkness. Laura had told me in the past, "He is literal fountain of ideas; he's created, designed, and patented numerous things. His scientific work, large optic lenses, is in use around the world." I imagine her sitting in the waiting room smiling at her "knight" who is searching for the grail that will cure her ills. She knows he is capable of creating plans, coming up with ideas, and calling in wild-brained colleagues. She feels if anyone can succeed, he can. I feel that Eugene must be desperately wrestling with the monster of disease and disorder that has sunk its teeth into the belly of his wife.

Laura says that when Eugene returned she realized that she was becoming unglued physically and mentally. "I had been holding myself together while he was gone. It felt like hours of sitting in the waiting room," she says. "I was feeling so cold and terribly uncomfortable with the pressure of the liver tumor pressing on my diaphragm. I could hardly breathe. I have begun to realize that this disease is really taking my life energy. It's really possible that I won't make it."

Denial is no longer effective. Laura is realizing that it is a matter of *when* she will die, not *if*.

She continues, "I felt time was slowing down. Finally a lovely young nurse gently beckoned me toward a hall leading to the conference room. My knees weakened as I started to rise. It was as if the animal in me 'knew' and was reluctant to enter a dangerous place. I was able to tell Gene how much really I need him, especially now. He held my hands to steady me and said loving things. He was so tender." I imagine that Eugene too was about to experience the shark of the disease, but he didn't fully know it yet.

Laura describes everything she saw and felt in the heightened state of mind that comes with holy terror. "Crossing the threshold into that conference room, I forget everything else. I was totally present. I remember every detail in that room: the smell of old coffee and stale air. I felt the enclosed space and the carpet under my shoes. I heard quiet sounds and murmured 'hellos' and papers shuffling. I saw all the doctors' faces, too somber, almost strained. I saw their clothing; most were wearing starched white coats, a few had rumpled coats. Some of the doctors were wearing what looked like happy, bright red bow ties, poking out of their white coats. How odd. I was aware of tasteful modern furniture, cream-colored walls with a single quiet green and blue abstract oil painting on the wall. I was aware of the golden light of the late afternoon spilling across the table. I knew that feeling of soft autumn golden light holding us all before the darkening of the winter.

We took our seats with them at the large rectangular, wooden conference table. I wished the table had been round, something curving, with a sense of eternity. Gene whispered something to me. I tried to take a deep breath."

I imagine Laura listening to the team of magnificently trained and respected physicians talking to her. They were explaining test results, weighing and offering choices of how, and if, she wants to proceed with treatment.

I imagine Laura and Eugene trying to be open to any path they are offering, willing to begin, almost like Hansel and Gretel, stepping onto that path leading into the dark woods. They had found their way through so many difficult challenges before. I know they saw the unhappy faces of the doctors.

Would they find a path out of the woods this time?

There does not appear to be enough time.

CHAPTER 22

Laura's Final Dream of the Analysis

Beginning of November of the seventh year of the analysis.

The day after the consultation with the team of specialists, after a long, after a sorrow filled drive, they arrive back at their farmhouse and retreat from the world. Laura and Eugene spend time together talking and slowly walking in the fields and woods. They begin to circle the nearly impossible discussion of their separation, the time when her death will come.

The prognosis is dire.

Initially the doctors considered surgery to remove the liver tumor or possibly perform a liver transplant-if she qualified. That would most likely mean weeks in an intensive care unit and a relatively low chance of survival. But when the results of the latest tests results were reviewed as a team; it was clear that Laura was not a candidate for a liver transplant. After an exhaustive study of all the blood tests, biopsies, and liver scans, the team of specialists had found that the cancer was highly aggressive, growing very rapidly; this tumor had wound around her hepatic artery. Surgery was out, not possible. The treatment offered was palliative care: comfort measures. They encouraged her to contact hospice as soon as possible. Laura will die from this illness, probably within six months.

Laura and Eugene, sharing a life, a bed, and an embrace of body and soul, will be married over a quarter of a century next month. They face what seems impossible: the inconceivable dilemma of final separation. We all practice this, like disaster planning, in any relationship. Over many years of marriage or partnership, many of us easily visit this dilemma in fantasy a thousand times. All this practice runs toward this moment: the time when the body does not continue its movements, its warmth, or even its murmuring sounds. Inconceivable questions arise. What sound does a couple make coming apart make? Ripping? Thudding? Tearing? Dissolving? Or is it silence? What is clear is that one partner becomes repossessed into the unknown and one is left dispossessed in the known physical world.

After Laura's "impossible" few days she has a dream of *terrible devastation*, which she shares with me in her phone session. I feel that this dream will be a message from her unconscious describing the devastation of her disease and her impending death. She writes it down in her dream notebook and makes a small pen drawing of a *bone set with precious stones and wound with strong, colored threads of silk.* She says she will send me a copy of the dream and the pen-and-ink drawing in the mail. When she shares this dream I know Laura is preparing herself for the unknown.

> *Dream: I've come to the aftermath of terrible devastation, where the people have experienced some great destruction, widespread loss of loved ones, an epidemic? I don't know if it's from war or disease. I think it is disease, because most of the mourners are men. I am being shown what the men do to heal their suffering and it's extraordinary. I think it must be in Japan. Many of the men I visit are Japanese. They are all working with utmost care carving and polishing the bones of their dead wives. The results are breathtakingly beautiful. I cannot speak when I see them. My eyes fill with tears and wonder. The men work silently, with reverence, as they smooth and polish, set precious stones in, and bind with strong, colored threads of silk, the bones of their loved ones.*

Upon hearing the dream I am astonished by the depth of beauty in this message from Laura's unconscious. I am moved, in awe, as Laura's psyche attempts to help her absorb the reality of *terrible devastation... great destruction* and guides her toward mourning.

Shaken by the powerful realities quickly unfolding; I am trying to find my way in this new territory...active dying has never been a part of my experience or my analytic training. I take notes, writing down what I can, as Laura tells the dream over the phone. At first, she talks about the dream as if it's about other people, another place, and another time, not here and now happening to her. I stay with her trains of thought as she tries to make sense of the dream's meaning and to cope with her overwhelming feelings.

She says, "The men in the dream are Japanese, survivors of war and disease, and survivors of the atomic bombings of Hiroshima and Nagasaki. They have experienced truly catastrophic events and losses. Yet their culture survived such unearthly devastation."

Laura associates the dream to her familiar experience, "Groups of Japanese men have come to our home many times for meetings to negotiate creative projects. I joined them for many dinners and evenings of discussions ranging from their arts to the effects of the war. When I went to Japan with Gene on business I studied the extraordinary craftsmanship and attention to exquisite detail in artwork. I feel that the Japanese men I knew could do what the dream is describing: ritual practices and putting their heart and spirit into their intricate arts."

I think it is disease, because most of the mourners are men. The dream is telling Laura that women, wives, have died from an unknown disease. Laura is being shown *what the men do to heal their suffering.* Her dream is assisting her with overwhelming realities, and helping her to prepare her husband for mourning. The dream is showing her something *breathtakingly beautiful and extraordinary,* evoking her *tears and wonder.* The adjectives she is using are of grand scale, indicating the personal *and* a greater collective experience. The catastrophe, the grief, and the beauty are taking place in an exalted realm of experience, in the archetypal realm of the Self. Laura *is* grieving through this dream and finding a way of acting in the face of annihilation: through creativity and imagination. Grief work can be profoundly creative. It is important that the work be performed with reverence: thoughtfully, carefully, and with a spiritual sense. The artisan's handwork gives grief a personally felt, nonverbal form, and a barely tolerable beauty.

Laura does not talk about this dream in the most personal sense, her death. She is a woman, a wife, dying. This seems too difficult; it is a blinding human reality. What she is capable of doing now is sharing this dream story, making a pen-and-ink drawing of a small bone set with precious stones and wound with a silk thread, and communicating it with me, her analyst.

Here is her early childhood nightmare manifest: *disembodiment, bodily destruction.* The heart of its meaning is simply too close, too unbearable. Sometimes the value and healing capacity of a dream is simply in the telling, in feeling heard and understood by another. I understand that this is what Laura needs now; to feel the profound impact of this rare dream is enough. I do not press Laura for more.

My mind revolves around the story and the images. I think about the wives' bones being set with precious stones. I remember the first dream of Laura's analysis almost eight years ago. In her initial dream, the stones, originally dark and opaque, have now become *precious stones,* small and creatively meaningful in a very human way, revered. In these last years I have observed that Laura has been living in a way that is allowing her to feel the preciousness of her life, and she is treating herself with reverence. There is linking and similarity of her early dream images of rough stones to the current, transmuted images of stones, which are now described as *precious.* These very valuable stones are formed under great pressure over time. This is the outcome of the hard psychological work of development and relatedness within her psyche, in her life. The men in the dream, the husbands, are in service of their wives as they *work with care* on the bones, binding them in *strong, colored threads of silk*. I feel this thread symbolizes the thread of life. Laura's psyche is organizing a story of images and behaviors guiding her and the dream figures toward wholeness, the Self. Her psyche has given her a message that the work is to be done is **by hand**, very personal and physical work. Psyche is showing her that the creative process of making art is a way, an ancient collective way, of expressing grief and gratitude for the lives of loved ones. This 'way' has been her way for a long time.

I remember that Laura treasured Native American weavings; she collected and used the colorful blankets over the years. In the Navajo culture blankets are woven with a "spirit line", a thread that goes beyond the ordered borders of the rug, which allows a way, a path for the spirit to leave. I'm remembering the use of thread for spiritual symbolism in other cultures: red thread, red silk or cotton is worn on the wrist or neck in China serving as an indication of spiritual and emotional attachment between loved ones. In Tibetan Buddhist practice, monks and students wear colorful silk cords for protection from negative or demonic forces and for positive connection their revered spiritual teachers.

In Laura's dream, the husbands' personal handwork is to bind, wrap and encircle the wife's bones with colored silk thread. This is archetypal in that this action is a response to the human experience of death and the honoring of the thread of life, now measured, and cut.

Bones are composed of calcium, the hardest, longest-lasting substance in our bodies. Universally, bones are experienced as powerful, even magical, and believed by many to carry the spirit of the deceased being. Some people perceive great spiritual power in religious relics, pieces of bone from holy persons. Bones decay slowly over great spans of time. Many cultures view bones as immortal, which means bones carry the possibility of *reanimation*. Reanimating the dead, or bringing back to life what appears dead, must begin with the bones.

It is apparent to me that analytic work has helped Laura deepen the meaning of her life and is helping her to approach death with awe, wonder and reverence. Laura and Eugene make their way towards the inevitable. One must care for the remains of the other. She reads this dream to Eugene. They wept together.

This dream becomes a vehicle for Laura and her husband to enter into the most difficult reality of talking about and facing profound loss. They approach that awful place: what to do with Laura's body after she has passed from mortal life. I believe Laura is speaking now in concrete terms about dying and helping prepare her husband for the moment she will be gone. The dream illustrates the creative work and sharing of grief with others as a communal way to bear and heal suffering. The work with the bones is performed collectively, similar to rites in many indigenous tribes. From her study and experiences, Laura knows the power of the circle in tribal ritual. The circle allows for each member to have an equal value and the chance for each to be witnessed. Symbolically, there is smooth continuity in a circle. Its roundness is often associated with the "feminine", eternity, and wholeness.

Death is a collective, archetypal event. Laura's circle of friends and family, the circle of humanity, will be held together not with *stones on a cord*, as in her first dream, but by the invisible thread of common grief.

And now, here it is for Laura.

We, like she, will die. Laura is facing her own divine catastrophe. This is the wholeness we are; we all experience life and death.

Laura's dream, which I refer to as "Polishing the Bones," remains one of the most beautiful I have ever heard. Dreaming, in my view, is one of the great arts of the soul. Laura's spirit will remain, her physical body will disintegrate. What was so intimate will become impersonal.

This is the final dream Laura and I will work on together in her analysis.

CHAPTER 23

What to Do With My Body?

A week later in November in the seventh year of analysis

How do I talk with Laura? She is dying. What does she want to do with her body? What is the soul? Does it depart? My mind has trouble wrapping around the idea of not existing, not being present.

Laura does talk about what to do with her body when the time comes. She chooses cremation. Eugene will take on the burden of this act of love, as many spouses do. He will carry out her wishes and will have a local woodworker, a craftsman, make a pine coffin. Her body will be held and carried and cremated in this coffin, a wooden container.

Laura tells me that Eugene went to meet the woodworker. He personally wants to make tiny wooden vessels for her ashes. The little vessels will be given to family and friends. Laura wants her ashes disbursed in the natural world. It is planned that the woodworker and his son will to deliver the coffin in several weeks. It will be set upon sawhorses in an empty room of the old carriage house. Years ago Eugene converted the space into a workshop. The tall workshop doors will remain shut.

Trees, the living symbol and body of the Great Mother, will provide the wooden boards that will cradle her body during its last days on earth. Nothing can save any of us from this reality; nothing stops death. We fall or float into death. This is our body for now; this is our temporary reality. Taking responsibility for our life includes what we do with our physical body when our life is over.

CHAPTER 24

Transitions and Entering Hospice

A few days later in November.

The general medical treatment for hepatic carcinoma would have been surgery, radiation, chemotherapy, and possibly a liver transplant, followed by recovery in an ICU of a hospital and maybe a stay in a rehabilitation center as well. This could have involved a very long stay, possibly weeks, in intensive care. All of this would have cost an enormous amount.

As it turns out, none of these medical treatments were viable options with Laura's particular diagnosis and the location of her tumor. Learning this, the couple begins to discuss the proposed palliative care. They decide that there will be no medical heroics, but there can be a creative and personal experience of dying at home surrounded by chosen loved ones.

Laura shares the conversations she has had with her husband. She chooses palliative care with hospice services. She wants to remain at home. The couple's health insurance, support systems, organizational acumen, personal financial resources and emotional resources allow them some flexibility. She decides against an expensive, elaborate casket, funeral, and burial.

Laura makes the decision to die at home. Being at home is so very personal. Many familiar people will offer their healing services, comforting Laura's body in this process. She expresses modest concern about pain control, nursing help, unexpected physical events such as bleeding or loss of bowel control, and difficulties breathing. She is intrepid. Eugene, who has his own similar concerns, fully supports her choice.

Laura's plan is to remain at home using every day and every hour to live as fully as possible. From what she has told me, her husband is a flexible, inquisitive man, an independent thinker, and gifted in assembling teams devoted to creative problem solving and projects. Laura's clear choice allows Eugene to be proactive and, although helpless to prevent his wife's death, he'll be able to express the best of himself with these actions. Laura and Eugene are a good team and are now facing the yoke of this challenge with some humor and growing positive energy. They are creating a very personal way to live into this final phase of their marriage and Laura's life. They are true to their life patterns of authenticity and acceptance of personal responsibility.

The psychological and professional relationship of Jungian psychoanalyst and patient that Laura and I have known for nearly eight years, and the analytic container, reaches its formal end with the diagnosis of terminal cancer and discussion of her final dream. We discuss a possibility of continuing her weekly telephone calls that would provide emotional support. I am expecting that Laura's life energy will soon be consumed by physical concerns and the needs of daily living. Our discussions will be more general and whatever is on Laura's mind at the moment. The in-depth analytic dream work, as we've known it, is complete. Her focus must change. Laura and I agree to conclude her analysis. With Laura's extremely rapid descent of health, termination was necessary, though more abrupt than either of us would have wanted. The formal analysis is over.

The next week passes quickly as Laura and Eugene begin to prepare for the unknowns ahead. Laura, in a long discussion with Eugene, has decided that she wants to ask me to continue to spend time with her, and with them as a couple, through her dying. She accepts that the formal analysis is over. They confer with each other about this possibility and agree.

Laura calls me to share what she and Eugene have discussed. She approaches me with her request, "Would you consider continuing to spend time with me, and be with us as a couple, through my dying? Is this possible? We are both inviting you to come here, to our home, and stay with us."

I am surprised. In analysis Laura and I discussed death(s) but we never imagined or expected her dying during our work. We never planned anything. I've never had a request like this nor have I ever imagined such a possibility.

The work they are requesting is to support them as Laura faces death. "With your help I want to review memories and dreams that I've already had. I want to prepare myself," she says. More than this, Laura is requesting that I be with her for her dying.

"I am moved, honored, Laura, that you would want me near. Let me think about your request. I need a few days think about this possibility," I say.

Feeling unsure of the correctness of this new role and path, I'm wondering if has anyone in my field has joined the journey into a patient's death in the manner she has suggested. I cannot find books or papers to guide me as I research this possibility. I know that if I agree I will need my own support system: my family and a senior colleague with whom I could express and process my experience during Laura's dying. I feel some anxiety with a lack of clarity in my role and I feel sadness. Then I realize that I also feel afraid of death itself. I speak with my closest intimates. An absolute change in the container and landscape of my relationship and work would happen. As I begin to face my fears, I begin to feel curiosity and a sense of the adventure that we'd all face and share together. The atmosphere of loss and grief will be ever present and, at times I'm sure very, very difficult to bear. There will be more, but of what? There are so many unknowns. A profound new learning experience was beginning.

I speak with my family, my senior clinical mentor, and my close colleagues. I speak friends who have lived through and been present at death, I speak with my other patients, informing them that there will be a significant change in my schedule for several months. They will be affected. This disruption will bring up issues for each of them. I am prepared to work through this disruption with them. I may loose patients. I know that many people close to me will be affected by my decision.

I do not have a clear idea of what lies ahead. I've never encountered this situation. I've been working in the field of mental health and psychotherapy for over thirty years. Though deeply grounded in human service, I consult with others and reflect on my thoughts and feelings. It is a risk: letting go of the structure of my relationship with Laura, as I have known it. Is this possible without letting go of deep integrity? The formal Jungian psychoanalytic work that I have learned and am comfortable with simply will not be big enough, not deeply humane enough, to help Laura in close proximity and with deep presence as she is dying.

What is ahead feels unorthodox and, I imagine, extremely demanding. I know that making this agreement is likely to lead my work and life into greater intimacy with Laura, Eugene, and others who are present during this time of great vulnerability. Dying is a very physical as well as spiritual experience. I trust the body and know that different kinds of experience and expression may come in the process of dying.

After great reflection I follow my intuition. I decide to agree to Laura's request.

We work out a contract.

The positive transference, trust, and intimate knowledge of Laura's inner life, which we had developed over the years of analysis, will continue through this supportive work. We will consciously, significantly, change the vessel or frame of our professional work together and the professional contract. Prior to and during Laura's analysis, I had never had any contact with her husband or family. I had never heard Eugene's voice on the phone.

Laura agrees that she and Eugene will personally pay for my travel, room, meals, and a negotiated salary weekly. I will travel back and forth across the country every other week and live with them for a week at a time.

This new role includes an airplane trip back and forth across the country every other week, and staying with them for a week. I make plane and car rental reservations, sometimes adding a night in an airport hotel during stormy winter weather.

Beginning in late November I fly round-trip to Boston. I arrange visits with dear friends, colleagues, and a senior clinician, all of whom participated in my decision. I go on to Vermont, to Laura's home. When I make the east I visit I stay with friends, visit colleagues and my supervisor. This is part of the way I care for myself: consultation, time staying with friends, eating well, rest, and relaxing with their support. This allows me to remain grounded in my own life and relationships while away from home.

From Boston I drive three hours to Laura's home. I live with her and her husband in their farmhouse during my week. I have my own bedroom in a spare bedroom/sewing room on the second floor. Laura is now living on the first floor, in her former den/ library near the kitchen. Eugene sleeps on the third floor in their attic bedroom. Laura is reaching out to close friends. She wants to address some unresolved feelings with several friends and family members. She invites them to visit and talk with her during this time of decline. Some of the time she asks me to sit and talk with her about her family, immediate issues, and the daily kinds of things- such as items of clothing she needs and, "What we will eat for dinner?" If she feels well enough we take short walks outside. We meditate together and, at times, I simply sit near her bedside as silent company. These become daily rituals. She takes comfort and pleasure in a small circle of caregivers that Eugene has formed. Practicing fluidity of plans and flexibility of mind and behavior is necessary, as change is always happening. The cooking and meals evolve. Eugene cooks and I learn what Laura can eat. Eugene shows me how he cooks delicious Indian recipes with fragrant spices, ghee (clarified butter), vegetables, and steamed rice. I begin to know him better as we work at the stove. I participate in food preparation and cooking, help setting the table or trays, serve, and wash dishes. We share all our meals together. I experience a deeper meaning of "companionship". The root of this word's meaning is "to share bread with." These meals become a form of communion.

I have a dream at the beginning of the change of my role and container of the relationship.

My dream: I join Laura and Eugene on a picnic in a lovely, warm tropical place. I am wearing light-green corduroy farmer overalls–comfortable working clothes. I can hear birds singing and water flowing in the background.

How can I have imagined a picnic at this time in their life? I reflect on my dream with unusual feelings of quiet joy. The light-green color of my clothing feels related to spring. The overalls are working clothing, humble and earthy, different from my professional persona or image. In fact, the overalls remind me of my work clothes when I was ten-years-old working a local riding stable, in my adolescence caring for my own horse, and later as a young adult, planting and tending my first vegetable garden. The overalls are the clothes representing the times I'm most close to the earth, animals, and plants. The dream setting is in nature with soothing sounds of water flowing and birdsong. My dream says that all is calm in the world; it's a "picnic", usually a time of relaxed social pleasure. This is an idyllic day in the country. The almost tropical setting and season seem a reference to a modest modern version of the Garden of Eden or Paradise. The dream contains my psychological compensation for the impending cold, harsh reality of winter in the Northeast and the coming of Laura's death and its proximity to Hades, the underworld. How can I imagine relaxing in the face of death? How can this be? My dream, my unconscious, indicates that this dying process might be far different from my conscious preconceptions, which are far dourer, sad, and filled with fear and misery. Clearly the dream is also a form of wish fulfillment and compensation. My psyche is trying to balance the coming realities.

The meaning of my dream becomes clearer as our communal meals become a form of feast, not so much in quantity of food, but in the quality of the gatherings of caring friends, caregivers, and family. Laura and Eugene are very generous hosts; I enjoy the emotional warmth and relaxation of these times. Evening becomes a time for storytelling and remembering. Laura and Eugene share memories from their travels and life experiences. The pleasure of simply being human together is deeply rewarding. We also review the day's events and address whatever Laura needs. The water of life flows through these hours.

I am not an expert, a teacher, or a superior, nor am I a guide. I am an invested companion and witness as Laura leads the way to her death.

CHAPTER 25

The Caregiving Circle Forms

It's now very late November. The leaves are gone. It's cold and damp and windy.

Laura has made the final decision to accept a referral for palliative care and hospice. Eugene calls the local physician associated with the hospice program and sets the process in motion immediately. Laura and Eugene ask me to be present during his home visit. The doctor arrives at 2 p.m. While taking off his overcoat; he nods appreciation for the warmth of the fire in the fireplace

Dr. Harrison is relaxed and radiates a sense of ease as he shakes hands with each of us. We meet in the first-floor library/den, which is now Laura's bedroom and meeting room. The doctor is early middle-aged, a bit overweight, and ever so slightly disheveled, that is, in comparison with Laura's description of the Mass. General physicians in their "red bow ties and mostly crisp white coats". I like him immediately. He has a heartfelt manner, a gentle and patient way of interviewing and listening. He shares a great deal of time and information during this visit. He explains the hospice system, the structure and plan of care, and what to expect from the nurses. He has brought the necessary forms to be signed. He raises the question of pain management directly. "Laura, it's critical to stay ahead of the pain," he says, "And I will help make this possible." He offers various drugs for comfort measures. With some anxious humor Laura and Eugene reminisce about living through the 1960s when many drugs and marijuana were illegal; they, like so many of their friends tried some. On a more serious note, Laura expresses reluctance to use any of these powerful drugs. She fears dependency. Since her cancer surgery, cobalt radiation, and hepatitis experiences thirty-six years ago she has used almost no medication, except the antibiotics for Lyme disease. She relies mainly on alternative medicine, comforting body treatments, and dedicated health practices. After a thorough discussion, Laura is able to allow for the possibility that she may need strong medication as time passes. She signs the *Do*

Not Resuscitate (DNR) order. Copies must to be kept on file with the hospice nurses, at home, and with the doctor. The stark reality of "no fluids, no feeding tubes, no emergency measures" touches us all. There is no going back, no turning around after walking on to this diving board into an ocean of unknowns. It is possible she could change her mind, but it feels unlikely.

Dr. Harrison assures Laura and Eugene that he can be reached by telephone and will readily treat various symptoms that will arise such as constipation, indigestion, and thrush, to name a few. Laura's immune system will become increasingly vulnerable as her liver cancer grows and continues to compress and strangle her hepatic portal vein. The toxins from hepatitis C and liver failure are accumulating in her body and stressing all her organ systems. Jaundice caused by her liver's inability to filter toxins will cause yellowing in her skin. This will become evident soon. The cancer will absorb her energy, all her life's force.

The doctor tells us about a special package that will arrive in a few days: a box a containing important medical emergency supplies, various drugs in tablets, two doses of morphine in small bottles, and hypodermic needles. Dr. Harrison explains the medicine: "One for anxiety, one for focus and mental stimulation, and the morphine is for immediate pain relief until the nurse can arrive."

Dr. Harrison asks, "Can you, Eugene, give your wife a shot in an emergency?"

"Yes," Eugene answers solemnly.

The doctor goes on. "When the box comes, store it on top of the refrigerator where it will be easily accessible." Further discussions about details go on. The appointment draws to a close; the doctor shakes our hands again on his way out. He has formally launched and blessed a mysterious private process, a strange adventure. Laura and Eugene have always been a good team facing challenges. They are quiet now.

The box arrives two days later. Eugene places it on top of the refrigerator as instructed.

With hospice services officially in place, the next pressing need is to find skilled nursing care for the days, and soon, the nights. It is late autumn; we are heading into the long holiday season. In this area, the choice of available, skilled practical nurses that are experienced with dying patients is extremely limited. Finding the best help during the demands of the holiday season and such short notice will be difficult. Winters here are snowy and Laura and Eugene's home is in a rural area with winding country roads. Whoever comes here during heavy snowfall must have a four-wheel-drive vehicle.

Eugene searches local listings. He calls some who are unavailable and finally locates a licensed practical nurse. She is at home when he calls and tells him that she is experienced, licensed, and has worked with hospice in the past. She explains that she recently assisted an older male patient and his family through his dying. It just so happens she, "Beverly", is now available. It seems that she is especially well suited. Then she adds, "I drive a four-wheel pickup truck."

Eugene telephones the hospice office is say that Beverly is his probable choice for a practical nurse. The senior nurse listens and remarks, "Yes she is licensed and did work for hospice in the past but we haven't used her in some time. She is no longer on our referral list." This is a delicate situation. The senior hospice nurse on Laura's case, Joanne Bentley, subtly warns him, without providing more information. She does not say more. The woman in question is in fact a licensed caregiver. Eugene, desperate for a nurse to be in the caring circle and on the schedule, believes that this woman is the only professional available in the area immediately. He calls Beverly to arrange an interview for the following morning.

In the morning, after a brief meeting with Eugene and Laura Beverly leaves. They found her to be cheery, energetic, neatly dressed, pleasant-looking, and a self-described "spiritually interested" woman. They agree to ask her to be part of the caregiving team. Eugene calls Beverly to offer her the position. Laura needs daily nursing and homecare help immediately. Beverly agrees and will begin tomorrow. Eugene decides that he can get other help later if needed.

Neither Laura nor Eugene has had the experience of being with someone dying. No one in this inner circle of caregivers, family and friends, including me, knows what issues will arise. Eugene and Laura are earnest, somewhat naïve under the circumstances, and are distracted by many details. Emotions and immediate physical needs do not allow the research and planning for nursing care they probably would have done under different circumstances.

Eugene can now make a schedule. He moves his business office from the local town, really a village, to the small room in the house just to the left of the library. A tiny bathroom is shared between the office and Laura's room. The small knotty pine paneled office has a phone, a fax machine, a large calendar, and lists of telephone numbers of caregivers, family, and friends. Familiar with the process of organizing working groups of people for his research projects, Eugene is competent and able to call on a community people for help, and local services for deliveries. He will make appointments with professional masseuses and a familiar chiropractor for Laura's care. He arranges a workman who assures them that the driveway will be plowed frequently to keep it open at all times. Friends volunteer to assist in grocery shopping. He sets a quiet rhythm for the day's meals and duties. I assist him in ordering additional bedding and cots for the family and friends who will be visiting over the holidays and beyond. There is extra room for accommodating guests in Laura's recently built art studio just across the driveway. Eugene is in full control now and has the responsibility of running the household. This will change as Laura becomes more incapacitated and is closer to death.

I help with any and all tasks, from the laundry to the cooking to going out for supplies. The house begins to feel like a base camp as we ready for the climb toward Laura's life completion and death. Getting practical things and matters in order now is important so we can turn our focus to Laura and all that her illness and psyche will require.

CHAPTER 26

Winter and Darkness Approach

Early December. Two months after her terminal diagnosis. Snow is falling daily.

Even though the weather is very cold outside, Laura asks for the windows to be opened in the mornings. She loves birds and wants to listen to the calls of ravens and the chirps of cardinals.

Several times a week in mid-morning a young woman house cleaner and plant tender comes briefly. She joins some of our morning conversations. Close friends call and visit intimately; some bring handmade offerings of love such as flowers or bread. The atmosphere is quiet and there is companionship throughout the days.

In late afternoon and in the night Laura rests and listens to CD recordings of songbirds. Laura especially loves the calls of Loons. I know these sounds evoke pleasant memories for her from her wilderness retreats. She finds the sounds and remembered images deeply soothing and calming. I find the loon calls sad and haunting, yet comforting.

Birds, nature spirits of the air, often associated with the unseen angelic realm, are present outside and in the home throughout the last weeks of Laura's life. Over the years many species of birds appeared regularly in her dreams.

Eugene takes time away from the house to run errands and pick up the daily mail at the local post office. He needs the fresh air and psychic space for his own reflection, private calls and meetings. Occasionally friends join for evening meals even though Laura eats very little. Samuel, her artist friend, comes to live here and assist for days at a time. He stays in a room in Eugene's renovated workshop. It is a short walk through the pinewoods.

Furniture is moved around in Laura's fairly large yet cozy room to make space for visitors. A fire is tended in her room around the clock for warmth, for the fragrance of burning hardwood and for the beauty of the flames. A cocooned, meditative space is created for Laura.

One day she asks me to place an order for a case of beautiful hand-made white vigil candles. She tells me the story of the Italian family from whom she originally bought these special hand made candles. They were very friendly with her when she was new to California. She has been a customer for years. I wonder to myself if this candle order is also her way of saying good-bye to this artisan family who shared her appreciation for the value of handmade art. There is little time before she will descend toward dying. A case of vigil candles is a gesture of hope.

Whatever work or task is needed, I offer my help: tending the fire, gathering books and journals, or finding specific fabrics or art material Laura wants to see or use. Mainly, I am as present as possible from about 8 a.m. to 8 p.m. Some late afternoons, when I'm not needed, I take time to walk in the woods. Sometimes I take a long hot bath on the second floor, the only bathtub in this old farmhouse. Immersing in water has always had the unique capacity to hold and soothe my entire being. Maybe it's my form of regression to the womb for a deep level of comfort and the physical surround that I need in the face of Laura's dying. These small retreats and making a hot cup of coffee for myself in late afternoon are important rituals of tending my own body and life. I am free to call my consultant whenever I need her support, and I speak to my family in Santa Fe in late evenings. I find that I have no interest in reading, writing, drawing, or any other distraction that takes my consciousness away from the present while I live here.

Laura, who was small before the illness, is steadily losing weight. She is now extremely thin and fragile and relies upon a cane for support. When slowly walking around the kitchen she pauses to look through the windows across the fields and stops to gaze at the little windowsill alters that she'd assembled over the years; her nature mementos are always central. She tenderly touches houseplants. Her dog Turtle wanders with her or is napping nearby. At the refrigerator photo gallery she lingers to study and remember the people and events in the pictures. Sometimes she speaks about the emotional history held in the images. I join her on the very slow little circular journey around the kitchen island; sometimes she moves on to the living room where Eugene can often be found napping on the couch. She stops to watch him sleep, carefully bends and kisses him on the forehead. We walk outside in the brisk cold on the snow-covered driveway. She loves the brisk fresh air, but it takes her longer and longer to dress, to bundle up. She becomes exhausted with the effort and cannot continue this ritual. She lets go of our outside walks. The circumference of her physical life is dwindling by the day although mentally she is very alert. Her demeanor is quiet, warm hearted, and gentle. She appears to be content. Her eyes are bright and clear, her pupils wide, somewhat dilated. So far, the oral medications and careful scheduling keeps her increasing pain under control. She doesn't complain and isn't exhibiting many symptoms of dire illness. There has been no need for emergency calls or the doctor.

Often I simply sit with Laura and sometimes, if they request it, I sit with her and Eugene. Evenings when Laura feels up to enjoying company, her friend Samuel joins. Eugene tells stories about their travel to the wilderness camp, to the Southwest, and to a Navajo reservation to purchase Laura's favorite colorful wool blankets. They are on her bed now.

Laura is sleeping less over this past month. I observe her in quiet reflective states more frequently. She seems to be meditating or attending to her inner world. On several occasions she invites Emma and Samuel to sit with us by the fire while she reads selected dreams aloud. These dreams are from her past dream work. She wants her close friends to hear how and when they appeared in her dreams. It's one of her ways of expressing how important they are in her life. This is first time I've participated in a "full circle" with a dream, that is, with its "characters" present and in dialogue with the dreamer about the dream work. The discussions that follow are a rich, moving and, a very creative way to honor relationship.

In the last few days she has reports seeing a flash of "something" outside her window. Her consciousness is changing, less process-centered or future-oriented; she is living more in the moment without asking for anything or searching for meaning. She meditates in late afternoons and evenings. I sit in meditation with her as she focuses on her breath or silence. Sometimes Eugene joins us, although the weeks I am there he is frequently in motion taking care of one thing or another. Action seems to help him cope with Laura's dying. I see him working, succeeding at making their home comfortable and functioning smoothly. He is skillfully protecting the peaceful, quiet atmosphere.

On the nights Laura is unable to sleep she drifts in and out of consciousness sometimes listening to Native American flute music or the sound vibrations of Tibetan crystal bowls. These are very simple, pure resonant sounds. She hardly reads and doesn't want to listen to the public radio station, both formerly favorite activities. She disregards most mail. She lets us know that many sounds or voices can become too stimulating. She does not want to hear any orchestral or choral music, only natural sounds. She is paring down to very quiet experiences that are more and more localized to her bedroom and tiny bathroom. It is not a time of thinking. Mental concepts and wordy conversation no longer interest her. She is living increasingly in a state of being.

She does not complain or command. Her eyes are clear, focused, and expressive. She is lucid and soft in her verbal requests. She expresses her wishes to control some things: "I like my water cup here … the temperature must be just warm … I need this pen here…this pillow needs to be higher … lower… the blanket is too heavy on my feet … the step stool by my bedside must be right here…this hot water bottle could use hotter water… Where is my little bell? We must keep it right here."

Moving very slowly, Laura is still able to dress herself. She only wears a simple loose outfit: a long-sleeved soft cotton shirt, very loose silk long johns, warm socks, and a red or blue soft wool shawl. She brushes her long hair into a ponytail and, preferring privacy, uses the bathroom alone. We are both aware that she could fall.

At her request now, I follow her up the narrow staircase and sit outside the upstairs bathroom door. She really wants to wash herself. There is no shower or tub on the first floor. She showers alone. Sitting on the floor outside of the bathroom door I realize that if she falls I will have to cross a boundary to gather and lift her naked body. She does not fall. I am relieved. Within the next few days the stairs become too difficult. Although a bedpan is brought home for her and offered, she has no intention of using it and never does. Self-contained and self-reliant, even now, near the end, Laura is able to continue to bathe herself in bed with a sponge and does not become incontinent. There is a tiny bathroom adjacent to her bedroom/library.

During her weekly visit Eugene and I voice some our fears with Joanne the hospice nurse She is a warm, very earthy woman who listens to us carefully. Eugene and I share a fear that there will be of some kind of dramatic bleeding. She explains what can happen: "Blood vessels can erupt within, causing a bleed-out through her mouth and nose." The highly experienced nurse speaks to us simply and practically, suggesting that we keep red colored towels on hand to use in this event. Eugene and I, neither of us with any experience assisting in a dying process, share a common fear that some kind of dramatic, bloody crisis will happen. Although Joanne does not expect this to happen, she is trying to calmly ease our overwhelming feelings about witnessing Laura's life spill out before our eyes.

Joanne spends time alone with Laura talking and examining her. After she says goodbye to Laura she walks outside with Eugene and me. We ask if she has a sense of how much time Laura has to live. The nurse wisely responds, "I can't say, every person is different." She is very relaxed and encourages us to enjoy the life there is for the few weeks or months ahead. "I will help you. Is there anything Laura wishes to do before her life is over?" she asks. "Laura did say she wanted to go with Eugene on a voyage in their retirement," I answer. Joanne tells us that it is not unusual to hear of hospice patients preparing for a "journey." She encourages us to support Laura's wish to imagine such a voyage. Joanne encouraged us not to worry about concrete details. Metaphors and imagination are welcome. It is highly unlikely that Laura was up to any physical travel whatsoever.

I am not feeling alone or afraid. I feel a deep sense of belonging, being an essential member of a group, a team, and a tribe surrounding a beloved and kind woman who is swiftly approaching the end of this life. Laura, Eugene, some caregivers, and I live in the cocoon of the archetypal realm of dying and service to the dying. This is holy work, holy experience. Undistracted concentration is a profound gift. I feel paring down to the essentials in life is a welcome relief. Simultaneously we are living in a hyper-vigilant state, alert and aware of changes in Laura's appearance or demeanor. This is a paradoxical experience of peacefulness and alert watchfulness. Laura managing her pain with oral medication so far now requests that the dosage be raised.

The days continue to revolve around meals—preparation, serving, eating and cleaning up. The time expands and dinner runs later and later, approaching 9 p.m. Laura eats ever smaller amounts, crumbs and sips. Each napkin, each tiny cup or plate on a tray is a small, pleasurable event. She loves being in quiet company. Her nourishment seems significantly less about the body and more about her heart and soul. This slowed expanded sense of time is deeply appreciated by Eugene as well. We gather around the little tray table near the fire in the hearth, near the lit vigil candles. I am aware of the irony that as Laura's death approaches, the couple is finally enjoying the pleasure of being together intensively after years work schedules that required their separation.

CHAPTER 27

The Eagle Dream Revisited

LOVE POEM TO GOD

I am circling around God,
around the ancient tower
and I have been circling for a thousand years,
and I still don't know if I am a falcon,
or a storm, or a great song.

Rainer Maria Rilke
The Book of Hours

Its mid December. Our relationship began nearly eight years ago.

Earlier this week Laura asked me to read a dream from our analytic work. She selects this one as particularly important. This afternoon Eugene and several dear friends assemble on comfortable chairs around Laura's bed. I sit cross-legged in a chair near the bed. Today she wants her pivotal *Eagle* dream read aloud while several of us are gathered. She explains to the others that she had this dream before she began her analysis. She dreamed this over eight years ago during a trip to the desert in the Southwest, months her decision to start analysis. She brought the dream to her analytic session a few months into her treatment. At that time she read it aloud with little feeling. We worked on its meaning.

She wants it read now.

Dream: In the desert. I am in a field facing west, in the West with others. The land is flat and I can see for miles except for places behind brush–sagebrush, tumbleweed, and mesquite. There are small groups of people scattered here and there. Suddenly I see an eagle with its wings completely outspread, falling straight to earth, surely to its death. There is blood on it, lots of it. It strikes the ground headfirst as it holds its wings rigidly away from its body. Everyone gasps both at the beauty of the creature, its size and perfection and the sight of its impending doom. But as soon as the bird hits the ground it soars back into the sky again, high up, rapidly, and we all see that a smaller bird, a hawk or falcon, is following it from the exact spot where the eagle struck. The smaller bird is also bloodied and the two do a ballet like this, repeating their rising and falling, following one another in turns. This is repeated two or three times. Each time the birds fall to earth, they are behind some vegetation and cannot be seen. The final time we see the eagle rise into the sky it is no longer followed by the falcon. There is a feeling of utter triumph, of freedom, and I realize that I am the eagle.

She is sitting up on the bed, spine straight, listening to the dream. Laura with eyes closed is deeply moved, fully emotionally engaged. We share a sense of gathering energy. She raises and opens her her arms, opens hands open wide, and breathing deeply her chest expands. Her eyes now open as she tilts her head back looking upward, her jaw relaxes and her mouth opens. She does not say anything. After some time, she exhales and returns to a normal posture. Smiling, with tears running down her face, she repeats, "I realize that I am the eagle!"

This time, so unlike nearly eight years ago in analysis when she quickly read through this dream unable to sink into her emotional feelings, she is consciously experiencing her emotion, embracing her spirit, becoming spirit in the form of an eagle.

Glory. That's what I felt while witnessing her experience. Just as her body is failing and literally wasting away, I sense her spirit ascending, releasing from the bounds of this earth and moving into the greater mystery. Although her physical body is still here, animated and engaged with us, part of her has entered another realm that I cannot know now. In her dream the eagle rises into the sky alone. Laura seems to intuit that she is beginning to leave us. She is preparing herself for the separation from this life and from us.

Much later that evening she asks Samuel and me to collaborate on a creative project. She asks me to write about the dream from her associations and discussions in our analysis. She wants to share her experience of emotional freedom close to the end of her life. She asks Samuel to create an etching from her dream's images. We both agree.

CHAPTER 28

Loss Lessons

Living close to and witnessing grief spilling from the hearts of Laura and her community, and remembering the grief of so many patients, friends, family, and feeling my own grief I write these lines while I am home in New Mexico.

LOSS LESSONS

I regret to inform you....
due to unfortunate collateral damage
...is no longer available.
Your access is denied.
The door closes in front of you.
The door closes behind you.
Your keys no longer work.
The number has been changed.
The matter is closed.
Your soul shatters.

No.

You are on this side and *it* is on the other side.
You stand in shock separate from your child, your body, your dream, your lover, your spouse, your friend, your home, your work, your answer, your sanity, and your future.
You stand, slump, then collapse in the disappearing face of the future as you had imagined it.
Like in a car accident, a violent blow or explosion, dismemberment happens all at once.
Utter silence in the place beyond the senses.
There are no words here.

CHAPTER 29

Surrendering

Christmas is coming in a few days.

Beverly, the woman hired to do practical nursing care over the holidays has been asked by Eugene to expand her service to include some nights while I am not living with them. So far, a full-time registered nurse is not needed when Eugene and I are both present. These are the weeks that the hospice nurse Joanne visits. There are friends visiting in the afternoons and Laura's friend Emma comes to help with daily tasks. She can assist in an emergency. A registered nurse named Jamie has very limited availability and is hired for nights during the weeks I'm here. She also has the necessary four-wheel drive vehicle. Eugene finds a full-time cook to take over the shopping and meal preparations for Laura and the caregivers. She is a cheerful, lovely young woman who is experienced in cooking natural foods and macrobiotic meals. She will make nutritious broths for Laura who can eat very little.

One day as the inevitable approaches, Eugene goes upstairs to be alone in a private room. I can hear his muffled weeping while I am downstairs in the kitchen. The weeping becomes sobbing. When he returns to the kitchen I acknowledge his grief gently. He is trying to protect Laura from his overwhelming grief. The following day he continues to have a very hard time containing his feelings and needs to cry privately. He lets me know he needs to go upstairs will be in Laura's former room. I hear his weeping, that becomes sobbing then I hear howling. The sound must travels through the floor. It would be impossible for Laura not to hear his agonized cries, his heart breaking.

Eugene's expression of the depth of his sorrow is important, and in my experience, unusual for a man. That he can express his feelings so deeply is a gift. I wish more men could allow this release. He is experiencing the loss of his beloved companion, feeling her leaving. He is holding still, facing and feeling his helplessness. After awhile his crying subsides. He comes downstairs and asks to talk quietly in the living room. He shares his dream from last night. Laura is going ahead, without me, into a cave. This is his psyche's clear message of dreaded separation. He cannot go with her now. Reality is hitting him hard. If Eugene was in a state of denial or avoidance of this reality, that is over.

His grief comes in waves week after week.

Current emotional losses open up our past losses. He is flooded. He doesn't talk with me about the details of his life. I am supportive and witnessing without questions or reflections. His crying seems to allow him to eventually rise from the floor, his bed, or the couch and go on for another day.

Laura is also expressing more emotional pain and sorrow with tears. She is mourning the loss of her life. Over the years of analysis Laura expressed great sadness and torrents of tears over 'roads not taken in this life'. She had sobbed with loss and regret many, many hours during her long analysis. Now, her crying is different, less gut wrenching sorrow. Now her tears are increasingly tender, like soft rain. I am present several times when she softly weeps in frustration with her physical discomfort, weakness, and sadness. This comes usually in the later evening.

She is mourning the loss of relationships with beloved members of her family, friends, her own body, and her life on this earth. In the morning Laura and Eugene discuss the lives of their blended family and their stepchildren. Asking me to be me present, they share regrets about their parenting and struggle to accept that some issues may not be resolved. They also share memories of happier family times.

Laura is not confined to bed. Mostly she sits up in bed or a chair nearby in her room. She still takes several walks around the first floor on most days.

Marital issues, part of what initially brought her into analysis, are no longer foreground. Laura told me that she returned to sleeping with Eugene within a year of her declared "time apart" in their home. She kept that separate bedroom for as a place to read, reflect, and journal. She stored her many dream journals there. She felt that the time she took assessing her life, apart from Eugene, yielded personal awareness, especially of her deep grief from childhood, her first marriage, and her health crises. In addition to a stronger marriage, the past years of introspection have also yielded stronger friendships, and heightened creativity.

Some sad realities can never be undone. Her grief over her incapacity to heal or change the course of a severe illness in one of her children is a living wound. She knows she can no longer shield her children or provide them with her relationship in this world. She is trying to come to terms with her earthly life.

Her family is flying home for Christmas. The social worker Laura had hired last year will accompany Karen for her last visit. As a mentally challenged adult, she doesn't have the capacity necessary to plan or carry out travel alone. It isn't clear how much she understands about Laura's health. Her beloved niece will arrive next week with her husband and young children.

By now the process of dying is demanding an enormous amount of energy. Laura's life force, her vitality, is nearly gone. She is letting go of her life. She is working to accept her losses and helplessness in making some things right in this lifetime. Discussions of politics, war, environmental issues and other collective issues she was interested in ceased weeks ago. Layers of former patterns of thoughts and interests have fallen away. She focuses on the immediate: the light of the day through the curtains, the presence of a friend in her room, the sound of a friend's voice on the telephone. I search for and locate a telephone headset for her. She barely has the strength to hold the receiver. She requires little: a warm cup of water, soft pillows under her back and head, a blanket, not too heavy, on her feet. The carefully kept medication log is open on the kitchen counter along with a pillbox of carefully arranged doses for hours and days. A month ago Laura would check the log and the pills on her walks around the house. She no longer gives attention to such details. The nurses pay close attention to the medication schedule and make sure Laura swallows the pills. Along with pain medication there are a number of over-the counter-drugs for discomforts of digestion and elimination, a common sides effect of pain medication. Thrush, the painful yeast infection in her mouth and throat, is a side effect of her weakening immune system.

Eugene had arranged to have a familiar and skilled masseuse come at least once a week. The masseuse offers gentle touch and "energy work." Laura is calmed and soothed physically and emotionally. At her request I am present, sitting silently nearby in the room during this bodywork. Laura is quiet; her body relaxes in this woman's skilled and caring hands.

My role has evolved into a quiet presence as she prepares to meet the greatest unknown. I sense a great tidal wave is not far away. Laura asks me, "Please, take all my journals and dream notebooks with you to keep." Laura and Eugene had given me full permission to write about her dreams, life, and dying. "I want you to use them if you decide to teach or write," Laura tells me. Following her instructions, I go to her former bedroom on the second floor. Neatly stacked at the back of her closet, I find many three-ring binders of her journals, all handwritten and well organized. Their covers indicate the chronological dates. As instructed, I remove them from the back of her closet and pack them in several boxes. I take them to the local Post Office and send the boxes to my home. I am deeply touched by her willingness to share the story of her life and her trust in me.

CHAPTER 30

At the Mercy of Caregivers

It's Laura's last Christmas.

In hospice care, here and elsewhere, familiarity naturally grows between the patient, family, and the various nurses. When I arrive every other week the routine is that the LPN Beverly, departs from the Laura's home about an hour or two later. That gives us time to check in and discuss anything. At this time Eugene, friends, practical night nurse Jamie, and I take over Laura's care.

Lately Beverly has begun to express her resentments that accumulated over the weeks. When I arrive from out of town she snaps at me verbally. If I'm having a private talk with Laura and Eugene, she comes in, wants to be included. She seems insensitive to the depth of intimacy in Laura's relationship with me. Laura and Eugene are friendly and warm with Beverly in the casual conversations of daily life, but they do not include her in their important talks together and with me.

Before she leaves one afternoon I notice something strange. Watching her I ask, "Why are you taking hairs from Laura's brush?" Beverly answers, "I'm making something with Laura's hair." I ask if she discussed this with Laura. "Not really," she says. I feel slightly disturbed by what seems to me, intrusive behavior. After departing, that evening Beverly leaves a long, angry message on my home telephone answering machine in Santa Fe outlining her complaints. I pick up my Santa Fe, NM home telephone messages at the end of the day from Laura's home.

The holidays are generally stressful for everyone.

Although the couple feels they need Beverly's services, her emotional intrusiveness is an increasing problem. Eugene speaks to me about his irritation with Beverly who began to use his very personal, pet name for his wife. He felt uncomfortable enough to address her directly, "Please do not use this name." He shared an incident with me. One afternoon the last week I was away, he had been napping on the couch in the living room, as was his habit. He groggily spoke affectionately to someone he assumed was Laura. He thought she had quietly come into the living room, stopped, and leaned over his head to whisper things or kiss him, something Laura did when she was up and able to roam the house. To his dismay, Beverly, pretending to be Laura, answered him affectionately. "I was startled, confused." He says, "Beverly's been acting a little weird, using my pet name for Laura, things like that, but this was too weird. After the couch incident he felt compelled to discuss this with Laura. When he does, she is distressed and starts to cry. They continue talking before taking any action such as firing. Eugene knows how much he and Laura have appreciated Beverly's practical care and dependability. Unfortunately her irresponsible, intrusive behavior is triggering additional emotional pain for the couple; it's too costly emotionally. Laura is aware that she's dying and that other women will enter Eugene's life sooner or later. This is a moment that pushes that reality too close for either of the couple to bear.

Beverly is continues to work for them after being admonished again by Eugene. The real problem is that he cannot locate another full-time nurse before Christmas. Tension is disturbing the peaceful atmosphere.

The Christmas holidays arrive with snow and cold. Two days before Christmas Eugene asks if I will drive into town with him for some errands. We rode in silence throughout the short twenty-minute ride. I was alone with him in the outside world and felt awkward. It is our first experience of being together in the world and, without Laura. We are sharing the intimacy of his wife's dying during a profoundly rich and painful time within their home. First we stop at a pharmacy for her prescription of oxycodone and search for over-the-counter medicines. Laura is struggling with constipation, a common side effect of pain medication, especially with morphine-derived drugs.

Laura is still using the oral form of pain medication. The week I was away, and tensions rising in their home, Dr. Harrison suggested a trial of Ativan, an anti-anxiety drug. She did try it but the side effects of that drug proved to be awful for her. I spoke with Laura by telephone and found her speech slurred and ideas unclear. She was losing the capacity to hold thoughts together. She and Eugene were alarmed. Ativan was stopped and her mental clarity and verbal capacities returned. Medications effect each patient's mood, physicality and personality, differently. So far, except for the trial of adding Ativan, Laura was receiving effective pain management. She is cooperative, takes medications, and she asks for increased pain control measures when needed. Her immune system is failing. Dr. Harrison has consented and supports her daily use of an herbal preparation from India for her immune system. It is not enough to prevent thrush from erupting in her mouth, throat, and intestines, but she wants to continue taking it. It's a bedtime ritual for her; before turning the lights off for the night, she mixes an herbal paste into a small glass of warm water. It has a familiar, sweet pleasant taste, and a spicy fragrance. Most importantly, it comforts her. The course of her dying is proceeding as Dr. Harrison had explained to them in the initial hospice meeting. Hospice doesn't provide the ongoing medications for increasing pain and other symptoms. If Dr. Harrison prescribes anything Eugene needs to pick up the prescriptions.

After collecting the items from the pharmacy shelves and having a brief talk with the pharmacist Eugene pays and we leave the gray fluorescent lights for the darkening winter light of late afternoon. Snow covers the street and landscape. We go a short distance and stop at a Christmas tree sales lot. I wait in the car while Eugene selects a fir tree. So very close to Christmas, the choice is limited. He retrieves a rope from the trunk and ties the tree onto the car's roof. This is the least joy I have ever experienced in carrying out a familiar, traditional ritual. I can see the sorrow in Eugene's face. Driving home there's no discussion; we look at each other with sadness.

Laura asked for the tree and wants to hang her beloved ornaments. Seeing and touching these things that hold precious memories for her this last time is important. Eugene goes to the attic to retrieve the boxes of decorations. Later that evening neighbors spontaneously arrive outside to sing Christmas carols for Laura. Welcoming them, although very weak, she stands wrapped in a Navajo blanket, leaning on the open door, her face beaming with joy, her tears falling. She is grateful for the gift of the carols, the neighbors, and the memories that rise with their voices.

I leave late tonight to drive to the airport hotel. I will catch an early morning flight arriving at my home on Christmas morning. Laura and Eugene will spend their anniversary day quietly reflecting on their marriage. Family arrives December 26th. I will return January first of the New Year.

CHAPTER 31

The New Yorker

New Year begins. January 1st 2001.

The January issue of *The New Yorker* magazine sits on a table beside us. Laura is a longtime subscriber, was a devoted reader for forty years. Laura had looked forward to its weekly arrival and savored *The New Yorker* magazine's cover, art, cartoons, essays, poetry, and stories. She had occasionally sent me *New Yorker* cartoons along with her dreams. Her subscription began during the time she lived and worked at her first job in New York City. Noticing the magazine for the first time today, she picks it up and has a look of surprise. The cover illustration is celebrating 2001, the New Year. Looking closely at the picture, she sees her personal history and her internal world of dreams coming together, arriving from the outer world, like a message from an unknown source. The picture uncannily echoes the central image in Laura's initial dream of analysis: there is a dark monolith rising out of the earth. She hadn't thought of that dream for years. Also on the cover was an image of diapered baby ringing in the New Year. Laura's series of significant baby dreams came in the second and third years of her analytic work. I sit near her bed to look at it with her. The picture includes a baby seated on the ground with its back to the viewer. The baby is wearing a ribbon banner, diaper and is holding a horn. The baby is facing the monolith, which is rising out of the earth. The baby's hand is reaching out to touch the large dark rectangular object. The baby's shadow is cast across the monolith. The cover celebrates the coming of the year 2001 and giving a nod to and referencing the celebrated 1968 film, and her favorite: *2001: A Space Odyssey.*

Viewing this image together, Laura and I look at each other and share a sense of this moment when her inner world of dreams is echoed and being mirrored in the outer world through this cover image.

Nearly eight years ago in her first analytic session she that felt her dream image of the monolith represented unearthing, the work of uncovering her self, her coming to consciousness. She was curious then about the mystery of the eternal stone. Such an object is an ancient symbol for the all encompassing Self. She also associated this image to the film, *2001: A Space Odyssey.* A year or so later in her analysis, the baby became a symbol for the neglected baby and child in her personal childhood. Later in her baby dreams, she was able to feel the conscious birth of the Self within, sometimes known as the second birth. Significantly, the baby on this *New Yorker* cover is depicted in a state of curiosity and wonder. This state is deeply familiar to Laura; her orientation to life and dreams is through a sense of curiosity and wonder. In the picture the baby's shadow is cast across the monolithic stone reminding us of its presence in all of us, as it must be, for our maturation.

For that moment, she is experiencing the image merging with her deeply meaningful past and present experiences. This is an experience of *synchronicity*, the term used by Carl Jung to describe an acausal occurrence of two meaningful events, or experiences, happening simultaneously.

Laura and I wordlessly share this *synchronicity*, during which one has a sense of being in the flow of life, a feeling of being part of a larger universe, mystery. This moment feels beyond simple coincidence and brings a form of affirmation and comfort.

The full journey of life including the approach of death is often depicted as a full circle. An ancient symbol, the *Uroboros,* is a serpent biting its own tail. This long known symbol represents the circle of eternal wholeness, beginning and ending utterly and forever connected.

The future has arrived. It's 2001.

CHAPTER 32

Making a Gift of Love for Her Granddaughter

Two weeks later.

As Laura edges closer to her death there has been no contact with the child that may or may not be Laura's own grandchild. Out of the blue, a letter arrives from Germany. Laura receives a card from the child's mother that expresses her sympathy for Laura's dire illness and shares a few details of her seven-year-old daughter's life and interests. There is no photo. Mark has acquiesced for his own private reasons and communicated Laura's critical condition to the child's mother. Relieved that her son yielded in this way, Laura is very happy and reads the note to me when I arrive. Keeping the card close to her, she rereads it a number of times. She learns that the little girl, Sabina, loves drawing and coloring, enjoys clothes, and playing dress-up. "She's a budding artist, another generation of women artists in this family lineage," Laura says. She feels that this note signals an opening, an opportunity, for communication. She feels the return address written on the envelope is an indirect invitation to respond. Laura contemplates her response and decides to make a many-layered gift for Sabina and will include a note for the child's mother. I understand that it will serve to communicate a great deal: much will be nonverbal, unwritten. For Laura, this gift needs to express a lifetime of love.

With her days and energy so limited, her response has to be formed into a single message. Laura decides what she needs for this project and she directs me to her sewing room upstairs and then across the driveway to her studio. She instructs me to gather Japanese fabrics she had collected over the years, a special piece of flannel, an illustrated children's book, and a tiny watercolor set she'd put away with a little pad which included a few completed watercolors she'd painted years ago. She is going to make a painting kit for the little girl.

Before my eyes, as I sit at Laura's bedside, a beautiful piece of printed Japanese cloth becomes the container, the way of an ancient Japanese custom. Cloth from her former fabric design work in New York City becomes the lining. She includes a small blue leather case holding a miniature set of watercolors, several brushes, a little water-color paper pad, and a tiny water bottle. The little watercolor paper pad still holds several tiny watercolor paintings made by Laura in Paris many years ago. She tucks a private short note in a flap of the leather case, which tells a story about the tiny paintings and a meeting with an older woman potter, the one who made cobalt blue pottery. She includes a small, illustrated book about turtles. Laura hand wraps each item in cloth. She writes and rewrites a short letter to Sabina and then one to the child's mother. She carefully ties the entire bundle with a Japanese knot. I put the bundle in a small box and seal it. She addresses it and asks me to take it to the post office. I do and it begins the journey across the ocean. It is a haiku of a gift: compact, precise, deeply orga-nized, and an artwork in itself. Laura completes this delicate, barely existent, relationship exchange. She hopes that her expression of care will be received. Outwardly she lets go of expectations. I know that she hopes that Sabina will draw and paint in the small watercolor pad and use the fabric to make clothes for her doll. This is a very important experience of emotional closure for Laura. This is all she can do. The effort has completely exhausted her.

Time is getting shorter. Relatives and friends are coming to visit. Jeanne Howell, Karen's social worker, returns for a very short visit accompanying Laura's daughter. Jeanne has agreed to be a temporary guardian. Laura felt that she was a warmhearted, responsible, profes-sional young woman with specialized skills in work with chronical-ly mentally ill: Karen. She is enrolled in an outpatient day-programs. Jeanne will continue to meet with Karen daily overseeing her day-care program, halfway house living situation, and medical services. So-cial Security Insurance (SSI) pays for Karen's services. Laura pays for Jeanne's social work. Eugene will carry on the responsibility of arranging for Karen's long-term care.

After her terminal diagnosis Laura talked with Karen on the phone about how seriously ill she was and told her that she would not live very long. Before they arrive for this January visit Jeanne communi-cated with Laura and Eugene with news that Karen has been easily an-gered and combative in her halfway home. This was worrisome. Laura thinks that this may be Karen's way of expressing distressing loss, her way of reacting to his impending loss. Karen and Jeanne are staying nearby at a friend's home that gives Karen time to see Laura, Eugene, and her brother Mark, who will be arriving soon by a van arranged at the airport. He's returned from Munich, Germany where he has relocated and is working.

Laura is tender and sweet with Karen, inviting her to sit with her on the bed. She seems calm and content being physically near her mother. Laura gently tells her that she will not be living very long, that this is their final visit. As Laura explains, Karen listens with no emotion. She does not, or cannot, dialogue although she can hug Laura, and does.

Mark arrives. There's a bed made up for him in Laura's studio, across the driveway. He plans to stay through his mother's last days, interacting with various relatives and spending time with Karen. Laura appears to be very pleased to have her children with her. I too feel very glad her children are here to see their mother and have this last opportunity to be together. Witnessing this tender family gathering, I know that they, similar to many families, are full of unexpressed complexity and emotional pain.

Laura's brother George, her niece's family, a few other extended family members, dear friends, and neighbors, all make very short visits today. Her niece's toddling baby girl is held in bed close to Laura, who is smiling and cooing. Eugene takes many photos of family members with Laura; he is capturing their smiling faces this last time.

The company has been a pleasure for Laura, now utterly exhausted. Most of the visitors leave. George is staying at a nearby friend's home. It is very clear to Laura's nurses and the circle of caregivers that these are Laura's last few days.

CHAPTER 33

Flight Home

It's the middle of the January, fully winter.

I am flying home to Santa Fe for a brief visit.

Miles above the earth I want to find words, a poem for the bone marrow of this experience.

FLIGHT HOME

By grace you are given ointments and friends to soothe your body and soul.
Images in your dreams draw you into the deepest mystery.
Approach.

Daily you sit at the loom of your life gathering threads of memories and organizing patterns.
You envision turtles swimming among strands of green and gold and silver.
You weave stories, dreams, and memories.
These are the threads of love.

Now your gift-bundle, containing the Turtle book, letter, and little paints, is securely tied.
Fabrics from a faraway place and time gather your greatest hope.
The gift is sent to a child, the one who emerged out of the blue.
You yearn to be her grandmother.
You hope she is another generation of women artists on your one cord.

The threads are visible in your genes.
The threads are in fabrics you designed, wove, selected, and folded.
The threads are in your dreams.
The gift is sent, like prayers, invisible into invisible.

This is all about faith.
You are becoming the cloth, the red silk of your dreams.

"*Wipe your tears on this cloth of red silk,*" says the wise old wom-
an in your dream.
Done.
Now we sit together at the table covered with the cloth of your
life.
You have become the feast, the host.
We each offer our prayers of thanks.
Silent gratitude falls like the light of ivory candles.
This is the vigil for the soul's journey,
moving beyond understanding.

CHAPTER 34

Letting Go

Late January.

Laura asks me to remain in the room during a visit with her son Mark. I met him for the first time recently. I feel awkward although I appreciate the clarity of her request: "Please stay with me now during Mark's visit." She is emotionally vulnerable and barely has the physical strength to sit up. Mark quietly enters her bedroom, approaches his mother and sits tentatively facing her. He doesn't question my presence, nor does he ask me to leave. There is tenderness on Laura's part, with no attempt to ask for anything. She is drinking him in with her eyes.

I sit quietly, witnessing a profoundly difficult moment unfolding in the lives of this mother and son. I've only known their relationship through her eyes and feelings, which Laura had shared with me over the years. This adult son was once so close to his mother in early childhood. He was a joy and comfort to her as a single parent. As the younger one, he had suffered greatly from the repeated separations from Laura during the time of her surgery, radiation treatments for cancer, and recovery from her hepatitis infection. When she finally returned home from the hospital, she told her young children of her decision to end the marriage. Their father would be leaving the family home. Another separation for the children, this time it's a separation from their father. Mark's sense of security had been shaken. Both their parents would become absent, or preoccupied by work and change. By the tender age of seven Mark was emotionally displaced when his mother fell in love with Eugene and planned to marry him. By adolescence, Mark had undergone trauma, confusion, and loss when his sister suffered a head injury in a car accident, fell into a severe depression, made a suicide attempt, and entered major psychological de-compensation. Both children essentially lost the sibling relationship that they had known. Laura has long felt Mark's lingering disappointment and anger. His distancing is very hard for her. She adored him and had talked about her feelings of shame for her failures in mothering and her inability to protect him from tragedies in his life. She felt that she could never give enough to make up for the losses of the past.

Over the years, Laura and Eugene visited Mark while traveling on business in Europe. He periodically came to stay with them in the United States. They maintained a relationship mainly by telephone. Mark had attended some college with their support and now worked as a writer. He was still trying to settle into his own path as an adult. Laura was excluded from much of the detail of his life over the last seven years. She struggled with the frustration of not being able to reach him many times, even in dreams. Some years ago Laura shared this dream,

I see Mark through a windowpane. I cannot reach him.

Now he here is at her bedside clearly caring for his mother. I sense how much he wants to keep his her alive, to keep an emotional connection with her. Laura rests against pillows; her body is emaciated. Her long hair pulled back in a ponytail. She's wearing loose cotton garments and a red shawl. She looks at her son with clear eyes that still hold the spark of brightness. He looks at her. With her belly swollen with fluids, "ascites"[11], she appears quite pregnant. What an illusion. Her body's capacity to retain peritoneal fluid at the cellular level is failing, signaling that death, not life, is coming.

It must be so difficult, even shocking for Mark to see his mother in this condition so close to dying. I sit in a chair away from the bed, silent and attentive, trying to honor Laura's wishes and being sensitive to his needs. Mark becomes agitated; he seems alarmed by her physical decline. Still sitting on the bed, he reaches for and grasps his mother's very thin hands, holding them tightly, then begins to on pull her arms. He is trying to pull her toward him. She is unable to respond. I feel the raw emotional energy in the room. No one speaks. Mark pleads with his mother's hands, eyes, and heart. Laura cannot speak. Unable to be still for very long, he lets go. He releases her hands, then moves to the foot of the bed and grasps his mother's uncovered feet. He keeps this position a moment and then shifts his fingers to touch her toes. He grasps both her feet again with both hands, finally letting go slowly of all but her big toes. He is holding on, clinging to his mother's body and her dwindling life force. I see and sense that he is expressing a primitive longing we all knew once.

I imagine words, if they could be used, "Mama, mama, I'm begging you not to leave me, don't leave me behind. I need you. I'm sorry. I love you. I'm not ready for you to go away," are never said aloud. Instead, there is a wordless, deeply physical beseeching.

I feel great empathy, sympathy.

We humans are mammals, *Homo sapiens*, and like all primates, we hold onto our mother with our mouth, fingers, hands, legs, and toes. Babies cling and pull at mother's body for safety, for food, for warmth, for security, for love and for the pure sense of skin-to-skin connection at its deepest level.

It is no different now.

I can barely describe the intensity, the tension that I feel being in this room: grief, longing, hunger, love, and fear. There is no peace.

Letting go of her toes gently, Mark gets up off the bed, turns, and walks away. His tall, slender body disappears as he closes the French doors on his way out. Laura, still not speaking, is now sunk in exhaustion with her eyes closed. I understand why she asked me to stay. It is agonizing for Laura to part with her children, no matter their ages, ways, or deeds. There is no resolution. There is only finality.

CHAPTER 35

Laura's Distress

End of January.

In the morning when I enter Laura's room I notice that she is unusually preoccupied and distressed. This is certainly understandable with this disease, the medication, the intensity of the family visits, and the activity in the house over the past days. Beverly is still working here; our schedules overlap with the approach of Laura's death. There is another night nurse but she cannot come every night.

I ask, "Would you like to talk?" She settles and wonders aloud about spiritual practices for dying. I say, "There are many ways to approach the transition into death though I'm not personally experienced."

Many years ago, at an elder friend, Jean's home in Cambridge, Massachusetts, I remember asking this same question of a young Tibetan lama, Tulku Thondup Rimpoche, a visiting scholar at the Divinity School at Harvard University. We were visiting this evening with our mutual friend Jean, who was extremely ill, a reoccurrence of breast cancer. She was moving toward death. I asked, "What can I do to be helpful to her?" He said, "Ask her what is important to her, support her wishes, and trust her." Two weeks later later Jean was actively dying, several of us who had been in a dream group with her for four years, were invited to meditate in her home at this time. Jean's daughter, at her mother's request, came downstairs to deliver her mother's last dream:

"I was being cocooned with a golden thread, the chrysalis placed in the crook of a tree."

Another of her friends who'd been on the Harvard faculty, Ram Dass, formerly known as Dr. Richard Alpert, was with her upstairs with her as she died. He described her peaceful crossing into death, "Her life passed into death like ink into water."

I ask Laura, "What would you want for yourself?" Laura expresses what is worrying her, "Beverly and I have been talking in the night; she is giving me detailed instructions about how to die 'correctly' if I want to be released from any unfinished relationships. She says there are things I must focus on when I am dying. I'm very worried I can't follow all the instructions."

I am stunned to learn that Beverly has been privately pressing Laura to use specific instructions in the moments before her death. I know that Laura feels unfinished emotional business with a few people. She is not sleeping well and while awake might want to talk with her night nurse. With Beverly's poor relational boundaries, Laura's vulnerability offers the opportunity for Beverly to direct Laura, using her own ideas about how to die.

Laura is increasingly agitated and anxious due, in part, to her failing liver; toxins are building up in her bloodstream, her brain. "I'm afraid that I won't be able to perform the instructions Beverly gave me to free myself," Laura says. Knowing Laura well, I feel that at this time of death's approach that Laura could feel like a helpless child. She is asking for instruction on how to "get it right." In her earlier life she struggled with "obedience to authority," outer authority. Now, at this most vulnerable time and under pressure, she is regressing. Deeply concerned, I encourage Laura to speak about her hope for resolutions with several people. The process of letting go of hope, accepting what we cannot control, and trusting ourselves is an enormous challenge for all of us. Laura's anxiety has brought important feelings to consciousness right now. The conversation is helpful to her. She is coming to terms with the painful reality that much is out of her control.

Later I speak privately with Eugene about the pressure and directives from Beverly and express my concern that this controlling and directive behavior is not helpful. Beverly's ideas and beliefs while they may be intended to be helpful, are intrusive under these circumstances. Laura is suffering from this "care". In fact, Laura and others who are very ill, especially the dying, can be unwittingly "trapped" with their caregivers. This vulnerability and anxiety can be especially real in the late hours of the night when a very ill person is awake with a caregiver, or during the times when family members need to be away from home leaving the ill person is alone with the caregiver.

Eugene asks Laura to speak about her conversations of the few last nights with Beverly. Eugene becomes very angry. Problems had been accumulating with Beverly's behavior for some time. There was already tension; this was the proverbial "last straw". Beverly is too much for them to deal with; she is inappropriately intrusive. The last thing Laura and Eugene need is managing this kind of behavior. He telephones Beverly who returns to their house. They go into the living room and he speaks to her about his mounting concerns. He terminates her employment immediately. She leaves noisily: banging the door and spinning her tires on the snow and gravel, speeding away. Shaken by the abrupt noisy departure, Laura exhales and expresses relief. Although this disruption is emotionally draining for all of us it has served to crystalize the heart of her fear, and Eugene's rage. He calls hospice and talks with their case manager Joanne Bentley explaining the situation and asking for more nursing help. In two days, the alternate night nurse, Jamie, will be able to help with additional hours. She is familiar, responsible, nondirective, and humble.

That evening Eugene and I reflect on the early concerns expressed by Joanne, the hospice nurse and case manager, regarding Beverly's behavior on other cases. Hospice had, in fact, removed Beverly from their referral list.

Now more than ever, Laura needs support to accept her life's completion, imperfect as it is, and to accept the death that is coming. She needs our respect in her process. She needs protection physically, mentally, emotionally, and spiritually. I deeply trust the wisdom of *her* life and *her soul's* preparation for this overwhelming transition out of life. I trust she will find *her way* if she is held lovingly by those closest to her heart. It is time to move on, with as little stress as possible.

CHAPTER 36

Vision of the Deer

Two days later, snow is expected.

Her brother George and son Mark have gone into town for supplies and errands.

Laura is emaciated, with a swollen belly, and boney. Yet she is radiant, almost beatific. Her body reminds me of the dream a year ago of a thin, boney, beautiful dark young man. In that dream she is with this beautiful man who must leave her. He says,

the moment comes when we must each stand and go our separate ways.

The failure of Laura's liver with the cascade of consequences for other organs is causing her extreme discomfort and agitation. Eugene calls and is advised by Dr. Harrison to increase the oral pain medication. He warns Eugene that this dosage of pain medication may diminish her capacity to communicate. Eugene immediately increases the dosage of medication.

We quickly see her mind and body loose coordination. When speech becomes too difficult, she signals for writing implements and struggles to write a note. I witness the ending of her ability to hold a pen to paper. Sixty-four years old, Laura has written daily since she was a small child. She created years of journals, took notes for hundreds of meetings and conversations, and loved drawing. Now she is in anguish, failing to form words on paper. This is her last attempt: she scribbles chaotic words. She writes, or at best, drags the pen: "I can think clearly!" The last sentence that she attempts to write unfurls, slants into hieroglyphics, the pen finally falling off the page. The tight curls of letters open up and a plumb line to an abyss is all we have left.

She can no longer hold the pen securely. Her brain cannot assemble the thoughts and impulses together. Her hands and tongue await instructions that cannot arrive. As though she is a prisoner inside a foreign jail, she fights for the capacity to communicate. She is forced into a new realm of communication that is unknown and, at this moment, frightening. So much adaptation is required so quickly. Increasing pain and agitation seem unbearable for Laura. Samuel is present. We are both anxious. Eugene seems in agony. He calls Dr. Harrison and hospice again. It is decided that since the nurse cannot arrive immediately, the time has come to open the emergency box provided by the doctor many weeks ago. Eugene quickly retrieves it from the top of the refrigerator. It contains two small containers of morphine, hypodermic needles and other pharmaceutical supplies that might help while we wait for a hospice nurse to arrive; she is delayed by the snowstorm. We are not aware of what's happening beyond this room.

With some fear and some bravery, Eugene administers an injection of morphine. I witness and support Laura and Eugene. I am greatly relieved that I am not in the role of decision-maker or the one required to administer the injection. A half hour passes. Laura's anxiety does not abate. I too feel helpless and anxious to comfort Laura. The hospice nurse finally arrives, assesses Laura's condition, and administers another injection of morphine. This is in addition to the oral, extended release oxycodone, the narcotic prescribed for the last weeks. The second injection eases Laura's pain and anxiety. The nurse now has time to introduce herself, "I'm Delores, the weather's terrible out there, I'm so sorry I took so long." She now begins to set up an intravenous line in Laura's hand. This is connected to a morphine pump that is placed close to her side. After a few minutes, although very weak, Laura is calming. She is alert and orients to her surroundings and the nurse. She acknowledges her appreciation with a slight smile.

First feeling relief, then I feel aching sorrow, and sinking in my belly. I know the act of starting a morphine pump is irreversible for Laura. Her overwhelming pain was unmanageable. Her liver simply cannot process any more toxins. Relying on the pump is a clear signal that she is moving rapidly toward death. Accepting the pump is as an act of surrender for her.

We are calmed with Laura's relief *and* the presence of this new nurse. Snow is falling heavily outside in deep night. Warmed by the freshly stoked fire in the hearth that is casting its soft light; I feel cocooned for a brief while. A surreal conversation unfolds. Delores, a large-bodied, salt-of-the earth nurse from hospice, becomes chatty as Laura's relaxation increases and her breathing less labored. Eugene, Samuel, and I breathe our own sighs of relief. Delores says, "In just a few weeks my daughter and I are going on a trip to Key West, Florida to go swimming in the ocean with dolphins." I think how incongruous this is and how wildly delightful to hear about such an adventure precisely at this moment. I remembered that Laura seriously considered this same adventure several years ago. I had been to the ocean many times to swim in the wild with dolphins. Delores' words are oddly synchronous in the midst of this dying time in the dead of winter. Just two weeks ago in this room, during one of our many conversations, Laura, Eugene, Emma, and I had talked about dolphins' extraordinary capacity to communicate. Over the years Laura and I had spoken of the mythology and mysterious social life in the world of cetaceans: dolphins and whales.

Only days before in this room her friend Emma had surprised me with a gift of a little, three inch sculptured ceramic animal from her personal collection. A professional artist, Emma had sculpted, painted and fired her creations in Laura's kiln. Emma said, "A gift in gratitude for your care of my dear friend Laura." Now, listening to Delores, the hospice nurse, I see the little sculpted dolphin hanging on a lamp just two feet away from Laura. It is gently swimming in the air on a clear-plastic string. I placed it there several days ago while playfully reminding Laura of this archetypal animal is known as a guide of souls into the afterlife. The little dolphin is now swaying over a small bronze sculpture of a female dancer made many years ago by Laura's mother. I feel the subtle ephemeral presence of spirit speaking through the mature, light-hearted nurse and through these artistic expressions. Thankfully Delores stays a while longer as we gather ourselves for the remainder of the night. Eventually she bundles up in her coat, boots, hat, and gloves and leaves in the dark. George and Mark, delayed by the weather, arrive back home very late. Eventually we each retreat to our rooms to rest. Eugene goes to sleep in the living room. Night nurse Jamie stays with Laura who is dozing.

Dawn comes.

Coming downstairs quietly I greet Laura, who is awake, and Jamie who is sitting by her side. Laura is able to get out of bed; using her cane for support, she walks slowly to her tiny bathroom with a knotty-pine Dutch door, just seventeen slow steps from her recently arranged bedroom on the first floor, Laura calculates by the hour her body's withdrawal from this world. With the mind of a chemist she uses a measuring cup to calculate the amount of fluids taken in and going out. She is not giving up hope. She glances up through the window toward the mountains freshly covered with snow. She calls me into the bathroom near her. In this moment she voluntarily drops to her knees; she whispers her vision, her epiphany: *"Oh! I see the deer!*

It is breaking through the snow and ice on the river and is drinking deeply from the cold water!"

The approach of her vision is swift, quiet, and filled with awesome beauty. A fleeting gentle creature of the earth and wind, the deer is sacred in so many ancient cultures. I know that Laura has been unable to eat or drink for days; she is starving and dehydrated, highly medicated, and is dying. Only Laura, who cherished the wild animals, can see this deer and river. This creature with its beauty and swiftness is precious to Laura. The ancient ones said that the deer is a herald of death.

Suddenly, in complete openness, she is passionately praying aloud for the earth and the rivers, for all lives, and the planet's well being. I stay near her in awe, in quiet, witnessing, hearing her wholehearted prayer.

Her physical strength gone now, Laura can no longer stand. Gentle night-helper Jamie and I are unable to lift her, fearing we might hurt her swollen, fluid-filled belly. Jamie summons Eugene from his brief sleep in the living room. Sleepily, he comes to tenderly lift her and carefully hold up the morphine pump now connected to her.

She rises slowly in his arms, standing on his feet. Here, in a dreamy dawn world, he, a knight in his pale blue bathrobe and she, his lady in her oversized silk pajama bottoms and cotton top, slowly move together across the room swaying, humming, and dancing. They dance regally to Laura's bed, where she comes to rest for her final hours of labor and liberation. I am watching the utter sweetness possible in human relationship. Here at this fragile time of great transition is the fruit of nearly three decades of a relationship, "the last dance."

Standing near, I am witnessing and remembering simultaneously part of a dream that Laura had shared with me years ago at the beginning of her Jungian analysis:

Dream: I am looking for a dance partner....

It is the last morning that Laura walks.

In early evening while Laura is dozing, a small group of caregivers including Eugene, her brother George, Mark, Samuel, Emma and me surround her bed quietly praying, meditating or simply in silence. Gently waking, Laura is aware of our presence and becomes deeply emotional. She seems to be experiencing something profound. Laura utters deep sounds, "Ahhhh. Ahhhhh" and weeps as if in awe of what she is experiencing, crying with soft tears, she slowly says, "This is more beautiful than I could have ever imagined."

I feel blessed being in Laura's presence at this moment and to be a part of such a compassionate group. We hold a quiet, reverent space for a period of time. One by one people express their love and by nightfall almost everyone returns to their rooms or leaves by car. Her brother sleeps in the studio near Mark tonight.

I sit near her bed in silence for a while until Laura falls asleep. Jamie, the night nurse, is on-duty again and settles into the other chair. I retreat upstairs to rest for several hours.

Unable to sleep I return downstairs and see that Laura is awake. Jamie is up and writing in the record-book, "Laura is awake. 6:00 a.m." Jamie tells me that Laura has just asked her, "Please go get the love of my life, my husband Gene." The nurse leaves to get Eugene who is sleeping again on the living room couch. He comes immediately. The hospice nurse instructed us on her last visit to look for any discoloration in her legs as a sign indicating that her circulation is ceasing. Jamie gently lifts the blanket to check her legs. Jamie, Eugene, and I see no obvious physical signs in Laura's body indicating her imminent death. Eugene settles and sits near her. We leave them alone together and close the French doors.

Samuel, sleeping on the bed in the kitchen, is now awake. Mark and George who had been sleeping in the studio enter the house. They both peek through the glass French doors into Laura's room. She appears to be sleeping. All is quiet. Mark and George quietly return to the kitchen and begin to make a small breakfast.

Everyone is talking with lowered voices, not wanting to disturb Laura who is sleeping. George expresses sadness that he and Laura didn't have more time together. Torn and conflicted: he wishes she could stay with Laura and he feels his need to return home to North Carolina. He's worried about his elderly wife and very anxious about the weather. His wife wasn't well enough to travel for this last visit with Laura. After calling the bus station to check the schedule George asks his nephew Mark if he could drive him into town this morning. He'll catch a bus that can take him to the airport. More snow is predicted for late today, which will make travel more challenging. After breakfast George says good-bye to us and signals his departure through the glass doors to Eugene and sleeping Laura. Mark carries the suitcase for his elderly uncle; they drive away. They had been gone an hour. Eugene invites me in and to sit with him near Laura. She stirs and turns in her bed. Awake, she very quietly asks me where Mark and George are. I tell her they've gone to the bus station.

Now, quickly and without obvious signs, Laura's final departure begins. Eugene, Samuel, and I gather closer to Laura. There is an atmosphere of heightened immediacy. For me, the energy in the room feels similar to the energy in the room of a birthing woman. The last hour of Laura's life seems imminent.

Laura speaks to us very softly and with great effort; "You have helped me in my life."

She is losing capacity to direct her life, something larger is moving toward completion now. Eugene, somewhat shocked, stands at the foot of the bed facing Laura. She indicates she wants to sit up. We adjust the pillows to help her. Samuel and I smooth blankets and sheets and secure pillows. Eugene holds her feet tenderly and faces her. I move onto the big bed on her right side, holding her hand. I breathe quietly with her. Samuel kneels at the bedside on her left, holding her hand. With her great swollen belly she appears to be a woman in labor, breathing, near to birthing. We surround Laura with stillness and quiet as she moves toward her final moments of this life. She looks toward Eugene and then shifts her gaze to a place beyond him, beyond our understanding.

Her liver is failing; her skin is rapidly becoming very yellow and her eyes are now golden yellow where the white used to be. We are breathing with her. Laura is now sunk deeply within herself, rhythmically breathing her way across an unfathomable expanse. There is no outer struggle. Fully jaundiced as she approaches her final minutes, I see two golden tears fall from her eyes. She is now transfixed into a far-seeing stare. Her presence is of another world. Momentarily, this woman appears to become a golden Hindu goddess, a Buddha. Breath by breath, each inspiration she makes becomes more and more shallow until, finally, there is a most gentle final exhalation.

In this last moment I feel a profound yet soft force of energy shooting out through her body, from her hands into ours. This force enters my hand, my arm, and moves through my body. Eugene folds over onto her feet. This moment is stunning, shocking, like being hit by soft lightening. I feel the Holy spirit move through me.

Stillness.

We are still here.

I feel a sense of incredulousness. The shock is mixed with terror, horror, relief, finality, and blessing. I feel high. I have never consciously felt this complex array of feelings all at once. I have never experienced anything quite like this before. I have never been in the presence of someone dying. It is all the more overwhelming for me with someone for whom I care deeply.

PART-III

Polishing the Bones

CHAPTER 37

After Death Rituals

I do not remember many of the things that happen in the next hours.

Hospice is called. The medical examiner comes soon after the nurse reports Laura's death. The doctor who arrives is an unfamiliar young woman. I am sitting on the bed with Laura's body; her face is not covered. This is the first time I experience such great physical intimacy with one who has died. I sit close to her body and touch her hand. I find no horror, only peace. The doctor silently lifts the sheet, gently examines her body and records the cause and time of death. I perceive that the hospice program staff was is in good communication with, and respected by, the medical examiner. I feel grateful that we, Eugene, Samuel, Jamie and me, are in this home, just a few quiet people, the dog, and Laura.

Eugene is permitted to keep her body in the home for several days by both the funeral director and the medical examiner. Someone places plastic sheeting, brought from a funeral home, beneath her body. There will be no undertaker or funeral home taking charge of her body. Her body is covered with a clean sheet. With the six large windows open, the room is approaching a freezing cold.

I am standing by the door, I see Eugene across the room carrying a basin of water to the table beside the bed. I stand by with Jamie outside the room. Under the sheet he removes old clothing and tenderly washes Laura's body, still soft, all the tension and weight of holding up a life now gone. He reaches to the nearby shelf by her bed for the red silk scarf and ties it around her head and jaw to keep her mouth closed. Her softness is quickly becoming inflexible, hard, *rigor mortis*. After carefully drying her body, he dresses her the in fresh simple clothing that Jamie set nearby. It's what she chose to wear in these last weeks. This age-old ritual, caring for the body of the dead, feels profoundly sacred.

Laura's peaceful dying and death are teaching me the meaning of "the incarnation of spirit in flesh." Death now unfolds before us with layers of subtle changes in her remains, which are rapidly drying and her skin is becoming pale. There are subtle shifts in her muscular expression. Without her breath, the fire within her body is essentially gone. Water within tissues is rapidly dehydrating. Her bones and, I feel, her spirit remain. In this quiet and still atmosphere, my instinctual wisdom feels Laura's body becoming *other*. She is no longer active in this earthly tribe. She now belongs to another world unknown to us.

I leave Laura's bedroom and begin reaching into the familiar world. I make several calls–the first one to Emma. "I've been waiting for you to call," she says. "I know Laura has died. She came to me in a dream early this morning. She was all pink, plump and radiant and said she felt wonderful, "as if I could walk forever," and she gave me a message for Gene, "Touch the back of his neck very gently," that's what she said. Oh, and a lovely dog, a Golden retriever like Turtle was there."

I have read and heard of such experiences; it is not unusual for very close friends and relatives to report such psychic visitations and dreams close to the death of a loved one.

Eugene is alone now with Laura's body. I hear a car in the driveway. Mark is returning from the bus station where he had taken his uncle hours ago. I meet him at the door. As he is entering Laura's dog Turtle races out of the house into the snow. Mark turns and chases the dog as I wait by the door in silence. They return. I quietly give him the news that his mother died a short while ago. He grasps the doorframe and sinks to the floor.

Turtle now sits by the bed near Laura's blanketed body.

Within a few hours there is a delivery of many fresh lilies and roses, white and pink, from who-knows-where on this snowy, cold New England day. I bring them to Laura's room. Eugene looks up, sees me holding an armful of flowers, and invites me in. I carefully lay the flowers on the Navajo blankets tucked around Laura's small body. I place single stems around her head and face, in her hair, by her sides, on her covered feet. Imperceptivity, the flowers are dying as I do this. Only hours before, Laura and the flowers were rooted to this earth. Without words Eugene and I begin changing the dying room into a vigil room. The cozy library, transformed to a bedroom, then a sick room, and a place for gathering, is now becoming a transitional and ritual space. The continuous fire in the hearth that offered soft light and warmth is now extinguished, the ashes swept away.

Eugene suddenly feels an urgency and quickly gathers anything that represents illness: the medicines, herbs, hot water bottles, rolling hospital table, Kleenex boxes, swabs, cane, little bell. He takes them out of the room. We pull curtains fully away from the windows, turn on lamps, and arrange more blankets. We remove end tables with various paraphernalia. Anything to do with hope for survival is removed. We light vigil candles, the ones Laura had bought two weeks ago. We change the space into a house for the dead, for Laura and her mourners.

In this time of tremendous loss, Eugene, like most of us, reaches out to do something familiar and comforting. He brings his camera into the room; he seems compelled to photograph the scene. Is this macabre? I move out of his way. I suddenly realize that he is *fixing the image,* holding on to the final image of his wife before he must let her body go. He is holding on to fleeting images, attempting to arrest the ephemeral afterlife moments, though this is impossible. Recording images of dead loved ones is generally socially prohibited. Our culture rarely shares such images. And maybe he is distancing himself from the shock. I continue to stand aside and watch. The answer is probably all these and more. We are in the presence of mystery.

CHAPTER 38

Vigil Days One, Two and Three

Vigil First Day

I know that according to ancient Tibetan Buddhist[12] practices[13], the space of three days after death is the traditional time period for the more subtle aspects of consciousness to depart from the body. At Eugene's request, we keep a vigil for Laura for three days.

We haven't discussed or planned the ritual or anything else that is unfolding. The ancient Buddhist ritual of the body remaining still for three days while consciousness dis-integrates on many subtle levels is not something Eugene learned formally. Yet this is what he is instinctively creating: time and place for the processes of the mind to dis-integrate. According to certain Buddhist teachings, ideas of who and what we are, and the "meaning of life," are mental constructions, not ultimate reality. For the deceased, these mental constructions continue and slowly disburse. The body ceases, but the mind takes more time.

I reflect on the spiritual and religious practices of meditation and prayer that Laura and I have shared in these last weeks. In our sessions over the years Laura spoke about and showed respect and curiosity for all spiritual things and ideas. In her final days life was a continuous spiritual experience. Laura, Eugene and I meditated together many hours. While sitting I experienced time becoming nonlinear, visions, and images in my mind. Laura and Eugene appeared as a couple from ancient China and later as Native Americans. I had the sense of many lifetimes behind their lives in Laura's last hours and moments.

These experiences simply emerged while accompanying the journey of a beloved human dying with respect and protected from the outside world. It seems that as her health and body disintegrated, her symbolic life, her spiritual life, become more real. My work with Laura's dreams and images was a bridge constructed over time to another, unknown dimension.

I feel the practices that Eugene sets in motion allow us, the circle of caregivers including Mark, to slow down. This gives us more time for reverence and helps to contain the experience of shock, and the grief yet to come.

When Eugene leaves the room, I stay with Laura's body as a witness and guardian. She remains lying on the bed, her face uncovered, her eyes closed, and her body covered with Navajo blankets and surrounded with flowers. The atmosphere is deeply peaceful. She appears beautiful in this natural death.

More chairs are brought in and arranged for visitors. Wrapping myself in blankets to stay warm I take up residence in a big easy chair and close to the library's French doors. I hold vigil in the chill of the cold room.

Emma, family, and friends who have been notified begin arriving at the house, each respectfully entering the room to sit with her body. Laura's niece returns that evening and wants to brush Laura's long hair. As she begins to separate Laura's hair into three large strands for braiding, another older woman friend arrives. She stands watching, and then asks if she can help with the braiding. A stepdaughter who had had arrived earlier offers to help as well. I witness this ancient rite of loving the body– paying last respects – treating death with honor. Three women, unafraid, tenderly brush and braid Laura's long hair. Theirs is a feminine, motherly, sisterly act of sending off, like preparing a daughter for school or church, for a maidenhood ceremony, or for a wedding.

Laura's "gown" is her treasured Navajo blankets. Rich colors: greens, reds, and oranges are woven in geometric patterns. I share the irrational feeling that the dead need blankets to keep warm, like a newborn's bunting and swaddling. Eugene moves in and out of the room over the hours.

Samuel, wrapped in a sleeping bag, takes the late night vigil in this cold sanctuary. We agree to accompany Laura's body as long as possible. I retreat to my room to sleep.

Vigil Second Day

This morning Eugene and Mark carry the pine coffin through the woods into the vigil room. Wrapped in blankets, Laura's body is placed by them into the handmade coffin, and set it upon sawhorses. Visitors bring small gifts and place them around Laura's body for the journey: a handmade cloth turtle, Emma's small porcelain figures of loons, a feather, a chocolate horse, poems, and a rolled drawing from Beverly, her former nurse. Family members include paintbrushes and paper, as she might need them in the next world, if and where it exists. Our small childlike gestures lay at the feet of the immensity of the unknown.

In the darkening winter evening, the group of caregivers from the last three months circles around Laura in her coffin. The candlelight and scents of flowers and incense surround us as we hold hands in the cold room. Several men lower the coffin to the floor. There I no longer see Laura, but I see a tiny old woman. She appears to be an ancient wise woman from any indigenous tribe, from anywhere in the world. It is as if the personal life fully transformed into the transpersonal in these last days and nights. The woman I knew in analysis no longer exists. We are living within an archetypal realm in a state of timelessness. We offer prayers as Eugene and others lower the lid of the wooden coffin. It closes with the sound of a complete fit. Eugene places and hammers the handmade wooden pegs. He made these with several close men friends in his workshop in these last weeks. The sound of the metal hammer on wood is hard, harsh, and final. He is closing the door to the past.

Vigil Third Day

The men place and slide the coffin into the bed of a pickup truck. Two of us, Sandra Eugene's youngest daughter, and I sit on either side of him in the back seat of an SUV. The procession of vehicles moves slowly on the snow covered backcountry roads. We drive between snow-blanketed fields. The world looks white. It is a bright, clear, cold and windy winter day. After arriving at the small crematorium of a rural cemetery, we gather together in a small cement and metal building.

There are tall sliding doors and a separate furnace room. Sandra brought the Bible that had belonged to Laura's father. She reads,

Who can find a virtuous woman? For her price is far above rubies.

The heart of her husband doth safely trust in her, so he shall have no need to spoil.

She will do him good and not evil all the days of her life.

She seeketh wool, and flax, and she worketh willingly with her hands.

Like merchant ships she bringeth her food from afar.

She stretcheth out her hand to the poor: yea, she reacheth forth her hands to the needy.

She openeth her mouth with wisdom; and in her tongue is the law of kindness.

Give her the fruit of her hands; and let her own works praise her in the gates.

Proverb 31:10,
The Holy Bible, Authorized King James Version.

Mark and several of the men now place Laura's coffin on the conveyer belt in front of the furnace. The crematorium attendant gently rolls it forward through the furnace doors. The doors will close before the cremation begins. It is Eugene, her husband, who will set the cremation burning process in motion. He presses the large red button igniting combustion. We are suddenly eclipsed by the great roaring sound of the blast. We fall to each other in embraces and tears. The fire of transformation is utterly real and final. Eugene staggers out of the building into the snow and falls to his knees by a tree. Several of us follow and sit with him as he weeps and the fires burns Laura's body to ashes. It will take all day, this burning. I'm told that the bones take the longest, the hardest substance of us. Eugene wants to be the one to receive the ashes. Mark will drive him back later.

Small groups gather and slowly and drive back to the farmhouse. In late afternoon Eugene tells us he will create a memorial service for Laura to be held in the spring.

Toward evening he and Mark drive back to the crematorium and return with Laura's ashes in a wooden box. The little ceramic birds, loons made by Emma are still there, nesting in the ash. They have survived their second fire. I touch the ashes in the box, still warm.

Tomorrow morning I will depart for my home in the Southwest.

CHAPTER 39

Departure and Divinity

It is said that if you take one step toward Him, He advances ten steps toward you.

But the complete truth is that God is always with you.

Mohammad

After the gathering.
After the dying.
After the death.
After the cremation.
After the rituals.

"After" is such a small word that seems so humble and exists between worlds. "After" implies some end has occurred. If there is an *after* then there must have been a *before*. I imagine there is a *beginning* on the way, somewhere.

I was in the "after" space, very low and very quiet, feeling that I'd left the earth's gravitational pull. Drifting like a feather, there is no going back and no falling either. Another world looms and we are not there yet.

Without the challenge of a snowstorm or evening darkness today, the drive from Laura's home to the airport begins with an easy, softly curving ride on two-lane country roads. For me, this is a time of reflection without engagement, without response. The countryside is rural even though the city is not so far away. This is a bucolic valley.

Once again I am returning to the Southwest, to Santa Fe, New Mexico. This time I will arrive home for an important family birthday. Weeks ago, when I returned home for Christmas, I felt that I was being given a pass to my personal life. This time is different. It's not the sacred dawn, nor is it the mysterious violet dusk, it is simply the day world in which everyone seems awake and life appears mundane in a subdued winter grey. I am leaving the archetypal realm of death and reentering the land of the living. Both are real worlds, each complete with landscape and language. Everyday life is largely predictable, horizontal. The steady rhythms of shopping, errands, and food preparation are comforting and routine for the fortunate. I am among the fortunate, a traveler between the landscape and the language of the inner and outer worlds.

Driving a rental car, a late-model boat of a vehicle, a dark red Chrysler Crown Victoria or something Imperial or Colonial; I am almost lost behind its large steering wheel. I picked a behemoth for safety in case of a snowstorm. I feel too small to be at the helm as it gently sways on the curves. I know this asphalt road. I know its well-placed signs, so unlike many roads in New Mexico where it can seem that you are on your own in a vast landscape of desert wilderness. Predictable New England signs are carefully guiding me to the airport.

Flying in and out of this airport, Boston's Logan International, not far from my former office, is a three-hour trip from Laura's home. For years, she had traveled to see me using that same three-hour round trip, twice a week for her analysis.

Now I, in a reversal, have been traveling to her at this end of our relationship. This trip from the high desert of New Mexico to the Green Mountains of Vermont and back is the one I have made every other week during these last three months of Laura's critical illness.

Driving, flying, walking, or running, really any movement through space, is simultaneously distracting and calming for me, allowing a shift out of one world – the realm of Laura dying – into another realm, my ongoing life. In my leased car, my private moving sanctuary, I feel held in a mystery of radiant quiet and calm, the calm that follows a storm of elemental experiences. I feel as if I am resting in a state of grace.

Without moving in my seat behind the wheel and never leaving the task of driving down the road, there is a simultaneous kinesthetic feeling of an enormous weight bearing down on my back and shoulders pushing me down. I am being lowered, being taught something profound. I feel myself bending in deep supplication, surrendering to crying. Slowly, with great care, I reach out to touch the invisible hem of a garment of an enormous being, a presence of numinosity. Holy. Holy. Holy. This is touching mystery. This is the reward of service to body and soul. The veil between worlds has parted for an eternal moment.

Here and now in this world, in a car on a road, these things can happen.

Somehow I must have returned the rental car. Somehow I must have checked in, arriving at the gate to fly to Minneapolis, the midway place. I am sitting at the spacious waiting area of Northwest Airlines with its large windows overlooking the snowy landscape beyond the runways on this cold February day.

I call home, my older son answers. His voice is an invisible kite string. I never hear the announcement for boarding. I never see all the people walking by to board. I watch the jet taxi, then speed down the runway and lift into the now blue sky.

I cannot say what startles me into realizing that I have just missed my flight home. In my entire life of hundreds of flights since babyhood I have never missed one, until now.

Somewhere between here and there, between worlds, I have let go.

The kind and helpful people will find a seat for me on a later flight. I will get home. No matter, there is no rush anymore. I am arriving, crossing over and back after touching another world, an "after" world. The journey home has begun.

It is said that if you take one step toward …

CHAPTER 40

Finding Laura's Last Dream

If a man could prove to some bird or animal that he was a worthy friend, it would share with him precious secrets and there would be formed bonds of loyalty never to be broken; the man would protect the right and life of the animal, and the animal would share with man his power, skill, and wisdom.

Standing Bear, *Land of the Spotted Eagle* [14]

Second week after Laura's death.

I am home after a journey like none other. I rest with my family, feeling blessed to be surrounded by those who love and care for me, for those who are alive. I walk on the high desert land with my dogs every morning and evening. The clear bright light of New Mexico in winter astonishes me; the great blue sky over the land is like heaven. The wild beauty is grounding.

I take time to read Laura's last dream journal from the boxes I had sent home weeks ago. I find that her dream journals are also dairies, each filled with dreams, sketches, observations, quotations, notes from conversations, doodles, and clipped pieces, articles and cartoons, from newspapers and the *New Yorker*.

Many creatures lived in the landscape of Laura's life and dreams. She had a particular fondness and affinity for birds. They frequently visited her dreams that she shared with me. They arrived in the form of owls, eagles, falcons and smaller birds with vividly colored feathers. The birds in Laura's dreams engaged in various activities: playing, battling, dancing together, drinking water or milk, even resting in the palm of her hand. In dreams, when trapped or wounded, the bird allows her to help. She sets them free.

I remember her telling me that whenever she found an intact dead bird in the woods she would wrap it in cloth, which she carried for this purpose. She stored her found "treasures", as she called them, in the kitchen freezer. Later, when there was time, she would make pencil studies of the birds and the patterns and designs within their feathers. She would always return their bodies to the woods.

From her last journal I now read this dream, which she had after we formally concluded her analysis. She had not shared this dream with me during my visits when we were no longer working analytically. She wrote it out and placed it in her last journal for me to find later.

*Dream: I come to the place where messages and mail have collected...
as I glance at the postcards: "We have stopped by several times to see
you but you've not been there." Who is this??? An unknown man comes
by. He is obviously "pushing" something. He comes to me and I know
I don't want to spend time with him. As he speaks he pushes a one-inch
high oval framed image of Christ into my hand and asks me if I will
accept it. I say, "Of course." The man looks relieved and moves on.
Later I am sitting on my cot with my lap piled with mail. The little Christ
souvenir slips down off my lap. I gather the mail together and lay it
together with some "treasured finds," the dead bodies of some small
rodents and bats. As soon as I lay down the mail, they (the creatures)
come to life...it's as if they have just awakened from a deep sleep. I'm
quite surprised and for a brief moment I wonder if this has anything to
do with my "accepting the Christ" token? I think this is silly but that I
cannot be sure. I am drawn to the animals and feel that they teach me
everything I need to know.*

This was a deeply personal message from her unconscious. There is urgency in it: *we have stopped by to see you several times.* There is an accumulation of postcard messages followed by the arrival of a male messenger.

I think about the archetypal "messengers" from the realm of the collective unconscious. In Greek mythology there is the god Hermes, in Roman mythology named Mercury or *Mercurius*. He is the traveler who can move in all realms, from Mount Olympus to the earth and to the underworld. Archetypal messengers in the Bible include the archangels Gabriel and Michael who were assumed to be from the heavenly realm sent by God to reveal impending archetypal events. The archangel Michael carries the message of the death of Abraham and the archangel Gabriel annunciates the Virgin birth. Native Americans understand the animals as messengers of the Great Spirit.

As far as I know, Laura did not have a *personal* relationship with Jesus or Christ as an adult. She practiced the values of Christianity and the philosophy of Buddhism quietly, privately, and was interested in and respected the values of other religions as well. But in this dream, the archetypal religious figure of Christ appears. She knew him in her early childhood Protestant church experience and through her father and his Bible. Laura's spirituality developed through her struggles; she sought to bring meaning out of suffering.

Here is Christ in one of her last dreams. She is offered a souvenir and accepts the image being pressed into her *hand*. She so valued her hands and all the work and art that she embraced with her hands. It isn't an ordinary mundane reminder of a time and place, but a remembrance of Christ, the holy man, teacher, and savior. I am reminded of dreams in which birds came into her hands. Creatures from the heavenly realm visited her, touched her physical being. In her last private dream she accepts the messenger's gift, the reminder of Christ, and *the man is relieved and moves on.* Our acceptance of a gift from psyche is very important even if we do not fully comprehend the meaning and purpose immediately.

Though Christianity may not have been a refuge for Laura in her adult life, she did not forsake her childhood love of Christ at the time near her death. In the depths of her soul she receives the message of Christ, a symbol of resurrection, a return to life after he suffered a torturous physical death and abandonment.

In this dream the dead animals, the *treasured finds* of nature, and the image of Christ combine on her lap and then slip to the floor. As these symbols come together the creatures awaken *as if they have just awakened from a deep sleep.* To her surprise, they are alive again.

Laura found *her individual spiritual way* by exploring the gifts of her life and soul. Through this dream, she received the inner guidance she needed, including the message of the possibility of resurrection. I feel instinctively that she faced the last weeks of life having received this instruction from within. It was not necessary for Laura to share this with me before her death.

I think she wanted me to show me that she, her psyche, had become her own teacher, no longer needing a therapist.

CHAPTER 41

Return for Laura's Memorial Gathering

It's been four months since Laura's death.

I have flown from New Mexico to Massachusetts and will drive to Vermont once again, this time flying over a different season. No more ice fishing scenes. No more whiteout snowstorms. It is the height of vibrant spring, all green, all Celtic. The mountains are lush. The earth is warm, soft and fragrant. Brooks flow, coursing through the meadows. It is another world apart from the snowy white stillness of the months Laura's life drew to a close day-by-day, hour-by-hour. Now is the time Eugene had planned for Laura's Memorial, the time for gathering of wide-flung family and friends. It is a time to see Laura's art, an astonishing and prolific exhibit, and to grieve. Under a large white tent by the woods, everyone will be invited to speak.

Arriving several days early to visit with the family members, I leave my suitcase, an unusually small one this time, in Laura's old room on the second floor. The room is the one given to me for this memorial visit. Many friends and family will be staying here using every available space. Although initially uncomfortable staying in this intimate space, this time I am here as a guest and am treated with generous hospitality. I am honored to be trusted with this space.

This is the room where, eight years ago, Laura made her stand to separate from her husband while reflecting on her life beyond the marital bed. In time, with her own inner work and Eugene's commitment to less all-consuming work in the world, and with a retirement plan imagined, they eventually returned to their attic room and again shared a bed. I think how, as with all marriages, there were issues and imperfections in Laura and Eugene's. And they were committed to their marriage and to each other.

This is the space where Laura had lived early on and later used as a study while she worked in much of her Jungian psychoanalysis, her therapy. I find stillness in the room, in the books, including many volumes of poetry. Many are familiar to me from our many conversations during treatment. They sit on shelves near the bedside, quietly present like dear old friends, just being there.

A poem can act as a compass, indicating direction in *a world gone upside down and turned inside out.* A poem can radiate some truth, some turning of the needle, which can indicate a way for a soul. I see Laura's copy of one of David Whyte's poetry books. As I reach for the book, it opens to her well-used and bookmarked place. I read,

THE WELL OF GRIEF

Those who will not slip beneath
the still surface on the well of grief,

turning downward through its blackwater
to the place we cannot breathe,

will never know the source from which we drink,
the secret water, cold and clear,

nor find in the darkness glimmering,
the small round coins,
thrown by those who wish for something else.

David Whyte[15]
Rivers Flow: New and Selected Poems

I remember the feeling of true North, the guidance of the North Star, or the divine, in his words. And I remember the feeling of the true South, the direction to the abyss: darkness, confusion and depression, places that we must visit on our way to completion of life. I think of Laura's early analysis that was saturated with depression and grief.

By the window there is a beautiful old watercolor by an unknown artist. It is painted with light-filled colors: soft blues, pale yellows, and peach. The subject is drawn by pen with India ink; an elegant woman is sitting at her dressing table. Maybe she's a turn of the century Gibson girl? The view from this second-story window overlooks a field of green grass, newly mowed for the event. I lift the window sash and smell the rich, sweet scent lingering in the air. Visible across the road is Laura's three-story art studio. It was one of the fruits of her life and her inner psychological work. Turning away from that view, I survey the closets with many built-in wooden drawers where, in her last weeks, Laura had instructed me to find the many journals that she wanted me to have before she died. She had placed them carefully in the back of

these closet drawers. She had expressed concern that there were journal entries that might be painful for others to read. Protecting others?
Protecting her? Probably both. I did what she had asked, boxing and
sending them to my home.

The floor, like many old farmhouses constructed of wide pine
planks, squeaks as I move about the room settling my things. Glanc-
ing through the door to the hall, my gaze travels across the long, low
shelves of books selected by Laura including her beloved collection
of illustrated children's books. Displayed on top of the shelves is a
series of eight framed photos that Laura had taken of the stray puppy,
Turtle, captured in various delightful antics. It was a winter many years
ago, when she had been lonely and depressed; she shared the story of
finding this puppy. She was filled with new excitement. Did Laura
see herself discovering her animal self, rescuing her instinctual life?
In the long months while her husband was away immersed in his own
creative work, Laura softened her isolation and loneliness with this
heart-warming companion.

On the bookshelf I see the Bible. It had been her father's and was
one of the very few objects that she had from her parents, both died
suddenly when Laura was in her twenties. I remember the biblical
reading on the morning of the cremation of Laura's body. ...*For her
price is far above rubies.*

I think about that word, *rubies* and my mind travels quickly to
rubies, red, rare and precious gems, from the Latin *rubedo*. In medieval alchemy this was the name of the sought-after, rare and valuable
achievement of an *earthly life in its fullness of love.* Ruby red describes
the fire and passion of blood, the incarnation of the soul in flesh on
earth, and the completion of earthly life. Rubies, real objects found
in the earth, become valuable jewels when revealed by the effort of
polishing. I am satisfied that the word *ruby* fits as a living symbol of
Laura's embodied soul.

I also remember the film *The Wizard of Oz*[16] made in 1939. Laura
was an impressionable young girl who loved films, was permitted to see
this and many other films while living on a military base during WWII.
The unusual heroine, Dorothy just a young girl, is given ruby-stud-
ded slippers. These are exquisite shoes that can magically transport
her home. Laura's imagination was her accessible vehicle, her ruby
slippers, and like her dreams, a gift from life itself. In the story, Glenda,
the Good Witch of the North, instructs young Dorothy to *realize what
she already has*: the capacity to wish and imagine. Dorothy uses her
gift and goes home.

The color red was prominent in many of Laura's dreams over the years.

After her art studio was completed she had this dream.

Dream: *Two crimson red birds have arrived, heralding the completion of my art studio. They have entered my space and are carrying a red silk banner.*

And from another dream, closer to her death: *...I was crying. A wise old woman let a brick red silk shirt float on the wind to me. The kind old woman suggested that it be used to wipe away tears of sorrow...the shirt then becomes compost. This is what we do here.*

Turning away from the books on the second floor I head down the narrow stairs. I stop in the kitchen briefly, passing through the space with the woodstove, now cold and empty. I reflect on the many intimate hours spent here.

The care-giving team long has dissolved and I no longer feel a sense of tribe. We are no longer a "vessel on a voyage to unknown places." As I come into the kitchen I see several unknown teenagers. They are *un-familiar* to me. I am not ready to meet new people, be social, not yet. I move by unnoticed while they play around, engaged with each other. I no longer belong here. The world has changed.

Crossing the gravel driveway, I pass the large, smooth, carefully placed rock and a purple-blue Siberian iris that Laura had planted and once painted in watercolor. I enter the first of three floors of her art studio. Constructed from old New England barn wood that had been collected and stored over the years; Laura imagined and designed this place working closely with Eugene, getting assistance from an architect, and working with a local builder. He became their dear friend. Word about this wonderful building had traveled through the community at the time of its completion. *Architectural Digest* had wanted to do a story. Laura objected. She enjoyed experiencing the materials and the construction, the adventure of the creative process, and she loved building a small community. She enjoyed the collaboration of creative, skilled people; she wasn't invested in notoriety.

Eugene assembled this exhibition, including many pieces new to me. It begins with Laura's early drawings, oil paintings, and some graphic prints. I see drawings from Laura's childhood including a delightful self-portrait in pencil. In the drawing she is about seven years old, stretched out on the floor on her belly, playing with a kitten.

As I climb up the stairs I hear classical music. The second floor invites the visitor into a spacious room flooded with natural light. I am overcome with a beautiful, extensive exhibition, a retrospection of Laura's work. Eugene, with help, had gathered and mounted the entire show. There's never been such a beautiful exhibition of Laura's extensive and prolific creative work.

Eugene and I meet with an embrace and a flood of tears. It is so good to see him. We are veterans of an archetypal experience: the realm of death. I am overcome with memories of the profound intimacy we had shared with Laura during the months of her dying. Here now, listening to the Italian tenor André Bocelli reaching for the heavens with his luminous voice, and surrounded by the astonishing creativity, I feel graced in a palpable, dizzying moment of sheer otherworldly beauty, breathtaking, and heartbreakingly beautiful.

I wish Laura were here.

There are many images, some published, of her fabric designs from years as a freelance textile designer. Long ago in an unusual moment of pride, Laura had said to me: "Do you remember the delicate Swiss-like flowers on flannel nightclothes? That was my design; I was in my late twenties living in New York and working in textiles."

I touch Laura's collections of shells, feathers and stones. Designs in nature are so discriminating, so subtle, and often highly functional. Who designed the multitudes of forms in nature? I know Laura loved their complexity and elegance, and took direction from these in her own designs. Photographs she'd made over the years are arranged in large frames, encircling the room. They are displayed by category, with each large frame holding numerous smaller images. Laura's interest in the beauty of form and pattern is obvious everywhere in her studio.

I go up another set of stairs to the third floor and see the wide-open area, also filled with natural light. There are several small areas: a work space with a curved, modern wooden desk, computer and chair, another space is covered with lovely rugs with a couch and chairs, a place for conversation, another area had a bed for guests. Across the room there are two vertical ten-by-four-foot hand-woven rugs are stretched on wooden frames. One is a golden phoenix on a red background and the other is a black and white loon floating peacefully on a lake. Although I knew of them and had seen photos, I'd not physically seen them. I find and read selections from her studies that she'd arranged in spiral bound books. I see that these contain carefully calculated mathematical patterns for her weavings and her architectural designs.

On a table in the center of the room are scrapbooks Laura made over the years of family photographs: mainly her children and stepchildren. The blended family gathered over many vacations and holidays. The last book of projects is filled with preliminary sketches of a retirement home that he and Laura envisioned. It also included drawings of a community center Laura imagined.

In a quiet area of the third floor of the studio near tall windows overlooking the woods, I find the dramatic three-by-four foot "Eagle Dream" etching made by Samuel. It is framed and displayed on a wooden stand with a framed copy of Laura's dream and my written thoughts. This is the fruit of the collaborative creation Laura conceived just weeks before her death. Displayed near easy chairs, one can sit to contemplate the dark, brooding images of winged raptors in dance, conflict, death, and ascension.

Preparing this exhibition was, and now is Eugene's way of remembering, honoring, and grieving his wife. His careful attention to artistic and visual detail is evident at every turn. The exhibit was carefully planned and beautifully presented. Eugene's care and reverence for Laura's creativity and life are apparent. He is fulfilling her wish of a gathering of friends and family to remember her life. The retrospective art exhibition was his idea and gave him, and others, the opportunity to view Laura's creative expression, the expression of her soul.

It is almost too much to imagine how one quiet, small woman created all this work. What mattered to Laura was not the awe-invoking feat of being an excellent, prolific artist; she barely exhibited her work. What really mattered to her was the *process of relationship*, her relationship to materials, to the earth, to her colleagues and teachers, to her family and community, to the creative process, and to her own soul.

As more family and friends gather, I return to the farmhouse. We sit at the dining-room table. We are no longer sharing meals here, as we did last winter. A large ceramic bowl in the middle of the table holds Laura's ashes mixed with wildflower seeds, sacred red earth from the *Sanctuario de Chimayo*, in northern New Mexico, and tree seeds. The communal activity now is to fill many handmade four-inch wooden containers. They'll be sealed with tiny wooden pegs. The talk is what I imagine of women from an earlier century at a quilting bee: quiet with soft laughter, friendly gestures and warm stories. This ritual with ashes evokes ancient funerary practices as we work with our hands, mixing together what was once a life together with the elements of nature. The containers are like tiny boats waiting to be filled. Each of us will leave the memorial gathering with some of Laura's ashes; we can participate in her return to nature as she had wished. The ashes will be scattered far and wide on the earth, in water, and in the air.

After an hour I retreat to the third-floor of Laura's studio. I want to go over my notes for her Memorial service. Eugene asked me to speak.

I sit at her desk in front of the computer that she rarely used, never really trusting its convenience. She found it mainly an irritant. She was a woman who loved pen, ink and paper, and preferred to trust her hands.

When beginning something of importance, I offer a prayer honoring and evoking ancestral spirits of the place and offer my gratitude for life. This ritual helps me to gather my courage before writing or speaking something that I feel is very important. Reviewing my notes I sink into my feelings in preparation for the memorial service just a day away. I write this draft:

Welcome to this community, the ancestors, and creatures of this place, those who came before us, the Native Americans, the pioneering settlers, the crows and cardinals, the squirrels and porcupines, the deer, the ladybugs, snakes and all the others. We take our place in the order of life, neither lesser nor greater than any other being. Interdependence, the weaving together of all forms of life, holds us in this moment. We are not alone. I give thanks for inclusion in such a graced and privileged circle of humans.

Searching for words, like mining for gold or diamonds, is a process of hard work, patience, and hope. Laura will always inspire me to reach for delight in the small, in the detail, as well as to reach for the glory in the grand, the emergent pattern. For her, everything and everyone became an aspect or a facet of the Divine. She passionately celebrated diversity.

Laura lived searching for truth that can only come from depth. I would imagine that Navajo elders, if they had known her, would say she walked "The Beauty Way, the Pollen Path". Golden pollen, the essence of the corn plant, symbolizes the essence of life itself. She attempted to bring consciousness to any situation and she honored beauty in everything.

For eight years I had the privilege of being a therapist, an analyst, a shepherd and confidant to Laura's soul. In her analysis we were guided and supported by the work of the Swiss psychiatrist, Carl Jung, a contemporary of Sigmund Freud. Philosophers, sages, mythologists, and anthropologists from many eras and parts of the world, in turn, guided Jung in his life and writings.

Several weeks ago I was reflecting on the words I would use today at this Memorial service. The partial text of a graduation speech delivered at St. John's College, appeared in my local newspaper. St. John's College in Santa Fe, NM is a small liberal arts college emphasizing scholarship in the humanities. There, students and faculty alike, study the literary texts of the humanities of Eastern and the Western cultures, in their original languages. These ancient languages touch many of us deeply and evoke the archetypal world. Sanskrit, the sacred language of the Asian ancients, is known as "the abode of the gods". Unknown to most of you, Laura had begun to study ancient Greek.

Dr. Cornel West, professor at Harvard and Princeton was the invited speaker at St. John's graduation and addressed the young graduates. I'm paraphrasing not quoting his words here:

Look deep into yourself for all history and social structure is there. The unexamined life is not worth living. The examined life is painful. To philosophize is to learn to die, to give up narrow perspective. Who has the courage to die? Do not sell your soul, negotiate and navigate this mass culture. I hope and pray you have the courage to free yourself, to fight for justice to create a better world.

How fitting these words feel. Laura has now graduated with full honors. She followed a path of individuation, self-reliance and self-reflection, without isolating from or abandoning others. She was devoted to the pursuit of truth and justice. Living with reverence for all life and giving unending attention to the detail and process of creativity, Laura did not sell her soul; she negotiated and navigated the mass culture. Attending only one year of college, for the rest of her life Laura remained a serious, methodical, and widely read student. She was to committed social activism, loved wisdom and, I feel, Laura learned to die. Taking direction from her own poetry, she learned "to curve inward toward the heart." She extended her capacities outward to many of us.

Her last three months were a time of harvesting the garden of her sixty-four years of life. It was a time of "honeying". (A word I create.) For the first time I am meeting many of the people who had long been a part of her life and dream world. We experienced the utter paradox of joy and sorrow day-by-day as we titrated pain and bliss. Dying at home is like being born at home, if it is possible, and it is not possible for many, and if there is courage and very good fortune, dying can be utterly natural. Both ends of the journeys are filled with absolute mystery.

CHAPTER 42

Glimpses of Goodness

Later in the day.

In the large tent rented for the purpose of the Memorial gathering, I am nearly the last of many who will rise to speak. I wear the dark red silk scarf around my neck, one worn by a stuffed animal I keep in my office, one that I had named "Bunny" as in the Easter Bunny. The animals help remind me, and many of us, of our roots in the body, the animal we are, and to appreciate the mysteries of fertility, sexuality, and motherhood.

Bunny acted as a psychological transitional object for Laura in her dying process. She kept its soft stuffed body near hers during the weeks I was away in Santa Fe. Eugene, family members, and friends took turns cuddling Bunny during those weeks, and Bunny was included in the vigil after Laura's death.

Today I want a private reminder of this soft transitional object that invites vulnerability, tenderness and bewilderment of the young child within each of us, who wishes to be seen and cherished.

It's time for me to stand and talk, to read what I have prepared to share. I go to the podium and stand there physically quaking. Suddenly, I surrender to my feelings and weep. Many gathered cry openly with me. All my preparation for this moment disappears. I am utterly sad. Instead, when I speak I share simply and honestly about the last night before Laura died when she consciously reached an experience of awe and numinosity. I share how we as a small group had supported and witnessed her in those hours of dying, surrounding her in what appeared to be Laura's ecstasy.

I assure the group that I believe that Laura indeed, consciously, reached *the goodness and peace we pray for*. I share a few moments of the extraordinary intimacy of those final days, Laura's epiphany, and the last photograph that Laura took last summer: a fuzzy, barely discernable mysterious image of a doe running away, into the dark forest.

Epilogue

The true partner is the mysterious and unknown "other" that moves within each of us throughout life and into death. Laura's willingness to risk having a relationship with me, using her analysis as a container and a resource that enabled her to reap the bounty of her dreams, the inner voice from the deep unconscious. Dreams arise out of our very nature. But first she had to be willing to unveil her inner life to another person. Laura had the instinct, courage, and resources to find someone who could "walk inward" with her, slowly listening and witnessing her life: the pain of being a complete human being with the inevitable challenges and disappointments of relationships and the reality of having a body with all its vulnerabilities. Laura consistently met life with curiosity and willingness to use her creativity. She sought the mystery of life and used whatever, whoever, brought her closer to this core of meaning.

Courage and fear are inseparable. The heart is the seat of courage, of spirit, and the nature of being human. Laura lived as fully as possible facing the unknown with help that came from deep within her soul.

The opportunity to work with Laura over many years was an honor and privilege. To know her as she was dying and through her death was a great blessing. A great confluence of experiences, ideas, creativity, work, and practice led to profound deepening of my life. I hope this story will similarly touch its readers. I express my deepest gratitude for Laura, the intimate sharing her life and death, and for asking me to teach from her dreams and her process of transformation. I thank her husband and family for their generosity of spirit in allowing me to share the last months of Laura's life and the hospitality of their home.

I thank my patients and my dear and supportive family for waiting for me to come home.

Notes

Introduction

1. Kübler-Ross, E. (1969). *On Death and Dying.* New York, NY: Macmillan: New York.
2. Saunders, C. and Baines, M. (1989). *Living with Dying: The Management of Terminal Disease.* London, UK: Oxford UP.
3. Becker, E. (1973). *The Denial of Death.* New York, NY: Free Press.
4. Meier, C. (1967). *Ancient Incubation and Modern Psychotherapy.* Evanston, IL: Northwestern UP.
5. Jung, C. G. (2009). *The Red Book.* S. Shamdashini, Ed. New York, NY: W.W. Norton & Co.

Chapter 4: First Dreams and Drawings

6. Griffin, S. (1993). *A Chorus of Stones.* San Francisco, CA: Harper.
7. Kubrick, S. (Producer and Director). (1968). *2001: A Space Odyssey.* (Motion Picture). California, USA: Metro-Goldwyn-Mayer (MGM).
8. C. G. Jung. (1953). CW, *Vol. 12: Psychology and Alchemy.* Princeton, NJ: Bollingen Series, Princeton University Press.
9. C. G. Jung. (1928-1979). *Collected Works.* Sir Walter Read, M. Fordham, and G. Adler, Eds. R. F. Hull, Trans. Princeton, NJ: Princeton University Press. Jung's commentary is wide ranging. He makes reference to any topic, animal, religion etc. throughout the Collected Works. (1979) Vol. 20, The Index, is quite helpful.

Chapter 9: Finding the Baby

10. C. G. Jung. (1928-1979). *Collected Works.* Sir Walter Read, M. Fordham, and G. Adler, Eds. R. F. Hull, Trans. Princeton, NJ: Princeton University Press. Jung's commentary is wide ranging.

He makes reference to any topic, animal, religion etc. throughout the Collected Works. (1979) Vol. 20, The Index is quite helpful.

Chapter 34: Letting Go

11. Ascites- a gastroenterological term for an accumulation of fluid in the peritoneal cavity due to severe liver disease.
12. Evans-Wentz, W. Y., Ed. (1969). *The Tibetan Book of the Dead.* London, UK: Oxford UP.
13. Sogyal, Rimpoche. (1992). *The Tibetan Book of Living and Dying.* San Francisco, CA: Harper.

Chapter 40: Finding Laura's Last Dream

14. Deloria, Jr., Vine. (2016). *C. G. Jung and the Sioux Traditions.* New Orleans, LA: Spring Journal, Inc.
15. Whyte, D. (2012). The Well of Grief, *River Flow: New and Selected Poems,* Langley, Washington: Many Rivers Press.
16. Thorpe, R. (Dir.)(1939). *Wizard of Oz.* (Motion Picture). California, Metro-Goldwyn-Mayer.

Bibliography

Albom, M. (1997). *Tuesdays With Morrie.* New York, NY: Doubleday.

Astrachan, G. (1999). Creating and Destroying: Dionysian Images of Dismemberment, Death, and Renewal. *Harvest: Journal for Jungian Studies* 45, 45-59.

Bach, S. (1977). *Guidelines for Reading and Evaluating Spontaneous Pictures.* Switzerland: Department of Pediatrics, University of Zurich and Clinic and Research Center for Jungian Psychology.

Baum, D. and Gallagher, D. (1987). Case Studies of Psychotherapy with Dying Persons. *Clinical Gerontologist,* 7, 41-50.

Becker, E. (1973). *The Denial of Death.* New York, NY: Free Press.

Bertoia, J. (1990). *Drawings From a Dying Child: A Case Study Approach.* (Masters thesis) 30: 0434, University of British Colombia, Canada.

Blackman, S. (2005). *Graceful Exits: How Great Beings Die.* Boston, MA: Shambala.

Bolen, J. S. (1996). *Close to the Bone: Life Threatening Illness and the Search for Meaning.* New York, NY: Simon & Schuster.

Bosnak, R. (1997). *Christopher's Dreams: Dreaming and Living with AIDS.* New York, NY: Dell.

Bowlby, J. (1980). *Attachment, Vol. 1.* New York, NY: Basic Books.

Bowlby, J. (1980). *Separation: Anxiety and Anger, Vol. 2.* New York, NY: Basic Books.

Bowlby, J. (1980). *Loss, Vol. 3.* New York, NY: Basic Books.

Butler, K. (2013). *Knocking On Heaven's Door: The Path to a Better Death.* New York, NY: Scribner.

Byock, I. (1996). The Nature of Suffering and the Nature of Opportunity at the End of Life. *Clinics in Geriatric Medicine.* 12, 237-51.

_____. (1997) *Dying Well: The Prospect of Growth at the End of Life.* New York, NY: Putnam/Riverhead.

_____. *Testimony to U.S. Congress: House of Representatives' Committee on Government Reform.* (October 1999). Washington, D.C.

Byock, I., Norris, K., Curtis, J. R., and Patrick, D. L. (2001). Improving End of Life Experience and Care in the Community: A Conceptual Framework. *Journal of Pain and Symptom Management,* 22(3), 759-77.

Caffery, T. (2000). The Whisper of Death: Psychology with a Dying Vietnam Veteran. *American Journal of Psychotherapy,* 54: 519-30.

Callahan, M. and Kelley, P. (1992). *Final Gifts: Understanding the Special Awareness, Needs, and Communications of the Dying.* New York, NY: Bantam Books.

Campbell, J. (1971). *The Portable Jung.* New York, NY: Viking Press.

_____. (1996). *The Hero With A Thousand Faces.* New York, NY: Meridian Books.

Chocinov, H. (2000). *Handbook of Psychiatry in Palliative Medicine.* New York, NY: Oxford UP.

Chopra, D. (2000). *How to Know God.* New York, NY: Random House.

Clukey, L. (1997). *Just Be There! The Experience of Anticipatory Grief* (doctoral dissertation). Rush University, College of Nursing. Chicago, IL. *DAI* 58: 1208.

Corbett, L. (1996). *The Religious Function of the Psyche.* London & New York, NY: Routledge.

Corr, C., Doka, K. and Kastenbaum, R. (1999). Dying and Its Interpreters: A Review of Selected Literature and Some Comments on the State of the Field. *Omega: Journal of Death and Dying,* 39: 239-59.

Dafter, R. (1990). Individuation in Illness. *Psychological Perspectives: A Journal of Jungian Thought Integrating Psyche: Soul, & Nature* 22: 24-37.

Deloria, Jr., Vine. (2016). *C. G. Jung and the Sioux Traditions.* New Orleans, LA: Spring Journal, Inc.

Dobratz, M. (1990). *Patterns of Psychological Adaptation in Death and Dying: A Causal*

Model and Exploratory Study (doctoral dissertation). University of San Diego, CA. *DAI* 51: 3320.

Edinger, E. (1985). *Anatomy of the Psyche: Alchemical Symbolism in Psychotherapy.* La Salle, IN: Open Court Press.

Eissler, K. (1955). *The Psychiatrist and the Dying Patient.* New York, NY: International Universities Press.

Eldred, D. (1982). *The Psychodynamics of the Dying Process: An Analysis of the Dreams and Paintings of a Terminally Ill Woman* (doctoral dissertation). Union for Experimenting Colleges and Universities, Antioch College, Ohio. *DAI* 48: 2778.

Elder, G. R. (1996). *The Body: An Encyclopedia of Archetypal Symbolism, Vol. 2.* Boston, MA & London: Shambala.

Eliade, M. (1954). *The Myth of the Eternal Return or, Cosmos and History.* New York, NY: Bollingen Foundation.

Erickson, E. (1980). *Identity and the Life Cycle.* New York, NY: W.W. Norton & Company.

Evans-Wentz, W. Y., Ed. (1969). *The Tibetan Book of the Dead.* London, UK: Oxford UP.

Fels, A. (2001). Cases: An Escort into the Land of Sickness. *New York Times,* July 3, https://nyt.com

Fein, E. (1997). Silent at Approach of Death: Talking Around Death and Hard Choices are Harder When Wishes are Unsaid. *New York Times,* March 5, https://nyt.com
_____. (1997). A Better Quality of Life, the Days Before Death, *New York Times,* May 4, https://nyt.com

Frankel, V. (1963). *Man's Search for Meaning: An Introduction to Logotherapy.* New York, NY: Pocket Books.
_____. (1967). *Psychology and Existentialism.* New York, NY: Washington Square Press.

Fraser, K. (1997). A Private Eye, Buddha's Flowering in America, An Inside View: The Great Matter of Death, *New York Times.* November 3, https://nyt.com

Freud, S. (1957). *Thoughts for the Times on War and Death.* Vol. 14. London, UK: Hogarth Press.
_____. (1962). *Civilization and Its Discontents.* James Strachey, Trans. New York, NY: W.W. Norton

Giessel, A. M. K. (1995). *The Role Hospice Assumed in the Twentieth Century American Medicine* (masters thesis), University of Texas at Galveston, Texas, *MAI* 33: 1400.

Goldstein, K. (1939). *The Organism.* New York, NY: American Book Company.

Griffin, S. (1993). *A Chorus of Stones.* San Francisco, CA: Harper.

Grof, S. and Halifax, J. (1978). *The Human Encounter with Death.* New York, NY: E. P. Dutton.

Groth-Marnat, G. (1977). *The Phenomenon of Dying as Seen Through the Dreams of Individuals with a Reduced Life Expectancy* (doctoral dissertation), California Professional School of Psychology, CA, *DAI* 38: 3880.

Gawande, A. (2014). *Being Human,* New York, NY, Metropolitan Books.

Hagen, C. (1997). Putting a Human Face on Death, *New York Times,* January 14. https://nyt.com

Halifax, J. (1997). *Teacher's Manual: Being with Dying Training Program.* Unpublished, Upaya Zen Center, Santa Fe, New Mexico.

Hamilton, E. (1942). Mythology. Boston, MA: Little, Brown and Company.

Hannah, B. (1971). *Striving Toward Wholeness.* New York, NY: Putnam's Sons.

_____. (1981). *Encounters With the Soul: Active Imagination as Developed by C.G. Jung.* Santa Monica, CA: Sigo Press.

Herman, J. (1992). *Trauma and Recovery: The Aftermath of Violence—From Domestic Abuse to Political Terror.* New York, NY: Basic Books.

_____. (2015). *Trauma and Recovery: With a New Epilogue by the Author.* New York, NY: Basic Books.

Herzog, E. (1966). *Psyche and Death: Death-Demons in Folklore, Myths and Modern Dreams.* David Cox and Eugene Rolfe, Trans. New York, NY: C. G. Jung Foundation.

His Holiness the 14th Dalai Lama. (1999). *Ethics for the New Millennium.* New York, NY: Riverhead Books.

Hoffman, J. (2016). A New Vision for Dreams of the Dying. *New York Times,* Feb. 2, http://nyt.ms/1Kn06vT

Hone, V. (1983). *Dreams as Preparation for Death: A Study of the Manifest and Latent Content of Dying,* (doctoral dissertation). The Wright Institute, Berkley, CA. *DAI* 44: 3528.

Hulsey, T. and Frost, C. (1995). Psychoanalytic Psychotherapy and the Tragic Sense of Life and Death, *Bulletin of the Menninger Clinic* 59: 145-159.

Jacobi, J. (1971). *Complex/Symbol/Archetype in the Psychology of C.G. Jung.* Princeton, NJ: Princeton UP.

_____. (1967). *The Way of Individuation.* New York, NY: Harcourt, Brace & World.

Jones, E. (1951). "An Unusual Case of Dying Together." *Essays in Applied Psychoanalysis 1:* 16-21. Hogarth Press: London.

Jung, C. G. (2009). *The Red Book.* S. Shamdashini, Ed. New York, NY: W.W. Norton & Co.

_____. Collected Works. Sir Walter Read, M. Fordham, and G. Adler, Eds. R. F. Hull, Trans. Princeton, NJ: Princeton University Press.

_____. (1957). *Vol. 1: Psychiatric Studies.*

_____. (1972). *Vol. 2: Experimental Researches.*

_____. (1960). *Vol. 3: Psychogenesis in Mental Disease.*

_____. (1961). *Vol. 4: Freud and Psychoanalysis.*

_____. (1956). *Vol. 5: Symbols of Transformation.*

_____. (1971). *Vol. 6: Psychological Types.*

_____. (1953). *Vol. 7: Two Essays on Analytical Psychology.*

_____. (1960). *Vol. 8: The Structure and Dynamics of the Psyche.*

_____. (1959). *Vol. 9i: The Archetypes and the Collective Unconscious.*

_____. (1959). *Vol. 9ii: Aion: Researches into the Phenomenology of the Self.*

_____. (1964). *Vol. 10: Civilization in Transition.*

_____. (1958). *Vol. 11: Psychology and Religion: East and West.*

_____. (1953). *Vol. 12: Psychology and Alchemy.*

_____. (1967). *Vol. 13: Alchemical Studies.*

_____. (1963). *Vol. 14: Mysterium Coniunctionis.*

_____. (1966). *Vol. 15: The Spirit in Man, Art and Literature.*

_____. (1954). *Vol. 16: The Practice of Psychotherapy.*

_____. (1954). *Vol. 17: The Development of the Personality.*

_____. (1928). *Contributions to Analytical Psychology.* New York, NY: Harcourt, Brace, & Co.

_____. A. Jaffe, Ed., (1963). *Memories, Dreams, Reflections.* New York, NY: Pantheon Books.

_____. (1933). *Modern Man in Search of a Soul.* New York, NY: Harcourt, Brace & Co.

_____. (1961). *Psychological Reflections.* J. Jacobi, Ed., New York, NY: Harper Torch Books.

_____. (1969). *Studies in Word Association.* Eder, M. Trans. New York, NY: Russell and Russell.

_____. (1965). *The Secret of the Golden Flower: A Chinese Book of Life.* Richard Wilhelm, Trans., New York, NY: Harcourt, Brace & Co.

Kapleau, P. (1971). *Wheel of Death: A Collection of Writings From Zen Buddhists and Other Sources on Dying-Death-Rebirth.* New York, NY: Harper & Row.

Kastenbaum, R. (2000). *The Psychology of Death.* New York, NY: Springer Publishing.

Kellehear, S. (1986). *Good Death: The Social Life of a Dying Person* (doctoral dissertation). University of New South Wales, Australia. *DAI* 48:0756.

Kessler, S. (1998). *The Dreams of Gay Men Living with HIV* (doctoral dissertation). California School of Professional Psychology, CA. *DAI* 59: 3063.

Kübler-Ross, E. (1969). *On Death and Dying.* New York, NY: Macmillan: New York.

_____. (1970). Psychotherapy for the Dying Patient. *Current Psychiatric Therapies* 5:110-17. J.H. Masserman, Ed. New York, NY: Grune & Stratton.

_____. (1975). *Death: the Final Stage of Growth.* Englewood Cliffs, NJ: Prentice Hall.

_____. (1978). *To Live Until We Say Goodbye.* Englewood Cliffs, NJ: Prentice Hall.

_____. (1981). *Living with Death and Dying.* New York, NY: Macmillan.

_____. (1997). *The Wheel of Life: A Memoir of Living and Dying.* New York, NY: Scribner.

Kiepenheuer, K. (1994). Illness as Oracle: Psychosomatic Symptoms as Synchronistic Occurences. *Images, Meanings and Connections:* 56-64. R. Goldstein, Ed. Switzerland: Daimon Verlag.

Levine, S. (1982). *Who Dies?* New York, NY: Doubleday.

LeShan, L. and LeShan. E. (1961). Psychotherapy and the Patient With a Limited Life Span. *Psychiatry: Journal for the Study of Interpersonal Processes* 24: 319-323.

_____. (1994). *Cancer as a Turning Point: A Handbook for People with Cancer, Their Families and Health Professionals.* New York, NY: Penguin Books.

Lockhart, R. (1970). Cancer in Myth and Dream: An Exploration Into the Relation Between Dreams and Disease. *Spring:* 1-26.

Longacher, C. (1997). *Facing Death and Finding Hope: A Guide to the Emotional and Spiritual Care of the Dying.* New York, NY: Doubleday.

Marrone, R. (1999). Dying, Mourning and Spirituality: A Psychological Perspective. *Death Studies,* 23:495-519.

Maslow, A. (1964). *Religions, Values and Peak Experience.* Columbus, OH: Ohio State UP

_____. (1968). *Toward a Psychology of Being.* New York, NY: John Wiley & Sons.

Mayer, E. (1994). Analysis of a Dying Patient and Some Reflections on Psychoanalytical Technique. Transactions of the Topeka Psychoanalytic Society: *Bulletin of the Menninger Clinic.* 58(3): 389-399.

_____. (1994). Some Implications for Psychoanalysis Drawn From Analysis of a Dying Patient. *Psychoanalytic Quarterly* 63:1-19.

Meier, C. (1967). *Ancient Incubation and Modern Psychotherapy.* Evanston, IL: Northwestern UP.

_____. (1986) *Soul and Body: Essays on the Theories of C G. Jung.* Santa Monica, CA: The Lapis Press.

Milch, R. and Schumacher, J. D. (2001). Dying in America. *The Santa Fe New Mexican,* Sept.

Miller, J. (1990). *Healing Loss Through the Exercise of Creativity* (doctoral dissertation) The Union Institute. Brattleboro, VT, *DAI* 51: 5018.

Miller, J. (1998). "Can We Die Not in Pain, Not in Fear? Dr. Peter Seluyn: Yale Professor and AIDS Program mentor." *New York Times,* Jan. 4. http://nyt.com

Mitchell, C. F. (2000). *Woman and Nature: Connection to Animals and Spirit Experienced by Celtic-Irish Women,* (doctoral dissertation) *DAI* 61:2274.

National Cancer Policy Board. (2000). American and Dying: 1999 Leading Causes of Death and What Matters Most at the End. *Journal of the American Medical Association,* Nov.

Neumann, E. (1956). *Amour and Psyche: The Psychic Development of the Feminine.* Manheim, R., Trans. New York, NY: Pantheon Books.

_____. (1976). The Psychological Meaning of Ritual. *Quadrant: Journal of the C. G. Jung Foundation for Analytical Psychology* 2: 5-34.

Norton, J. (1963). Treatment of a Dying Patient. *The Psychological Treatment of the Child.* Vol. 18: 541-560.

Nuland, S. (1994). *How We Die.* New York, NY: Alfred A. Knopf.

Oliver, M. (1992). *New and Selected Poems.* Boston, MA: Beacon Press.

_____. (2009). Red Bird Explains Himself. *Red Bird.* Boston, MA: Beacon Press.

Onions, C.T., Ed. (1966). *The Oxford Dictionary of English Etymology.* London, UK: Oxford UP: London.

Orbach, A. (1998). Not Too Late: Psychotherapy and Aging. *International Journal of Psychotherapy* 3: 94-6.

Palmer, G. (1999). *Disclosure and Assimilation of Exceptional Human Experiences: Meaningful, Transformative and Spiritual Aspects (doctoral dissertation).* DAI 60:2358.

Pattison, E. M. (1977). *The Experience of Dying.* Englewood Cliffs, NJ: Prentice-Hall.

Pennington, M. (1982). *Living or Dying: An Investigation of the Balance Point.* Canada: University of Toronto, DAI 44: 0441.

Perroux, F. (1954). The Gift: Its Economic Meaning in Contemporary Capitalism. *Diogenes* 6: 1-21, Spring.

Prendergast, J. (1986). *Dreams by Persons with Life-Threatening Illness: Death, Rebirth, Dying, Terminal, and Meditation* (doctoral dissertation). Berkley, CA: California Institute of Integral Studies. DAI 47: 3122.

Riley, I. (1999). *Transformation: Through the Process of Bereavement and the Use of the Spirit* (doctoral dissertation) DAI 60: 2364.

Rilke, R. M. (2005). Love Poems to God. *The Book of Hours*, New York, NY: Penguin Books.

Rizzolo, C. (2011). *Illuminating the Twilight* (doctoral dissertation). Carpentaria, CA: Pacifica Graduate Institute of Psychology.

Rosenthal, H. (1957). Psychotherapy for the Dying. *American Journal of Psychother-apy,* 11, 626-633.62

Ruitenbeck, M., Ed. (1969). *Death: Interpretations.* New York, NY: Dell.

Sacks, O. (2015). Oliver Sacks at Eighty. Essay. *New York Times*, July 7. http://nyt.com.

St. Clair, M. (2000). An Unfortunate Family: Terminal Illness and the Altering of the Attachment Bond. *American Journal of Psychotherapy* 54(4): 512-18.

Sankar, A. (1999). *Dying at Home: A Family Guide for Caregiving.* Baltimore, MD: Johns Hopkins UP.

Saunders, C. and Baines, M. (1989). *Living with Dying: The Management of Terminal Disease.* London, UK: Oxford UP.

Schroeder-Sheker, T. (1993). On Music for the Dying. *Advances: The Journal of Mind-Body Health.* 9: 36-48.

Singer, J. (1994). *Boundaries of the Soul.* New York, NY: Doubleday.

Simonton, C., Matthews-Simonton, S., and Creighton, J. (1980). *Getting Well Again: A Step-by-Step Self-Help Guide to Overcoming Cancer for Patients and Their Families.* New York, NY: Bantam: New York.

Siegel, B. (1986). *Love, Medicine and Miracles: Lessons Learned About Self-Help from a Surgeon's Experience with Exceptional Patients.* New York, NY: Harper & Row.

Schachter, S. (1999). *The Experience of Living with a Life-Threatening Illness: A Phe-nomenological Study of Dying Cancer Patients and Their Family Caregivers.* New York: The Union Institute. DAI 60: 3205.

Seigel, D. (2000). The Developing Mind and the Resolution of Trauma: Some Ideas About Information Processing and an Interpersonal Neurobiology of Psychology. *Paradigm Prism.* Francine Shapiro, Ed. Washington, D. C.: APA Press.

Seigel, D. (2001). Toward an Interpersonal Neurobiology of the Developing Mind: Attachment Relationships, 'Mindsight,' and Neural Integration. *Infant Mental Health Journal* 22(1-2): 67-94.

Singh, K. D. (1998). *The Grace in Dying: How We Are Transformed Spiritually as We Die.* San Francisco, CA: Harper.

Sogyal, Rimpoche. (1992). *The Tibetan Book of Living and Dying.* San Francisco, CA: Harper.

Smith, C. (1990). *Indistinguishable From the Darkness.* New York, NY: W.W. Norton & Co.

Stedeford, A. (1979). Psychotherapy of the Dying Patient. *British Journal of Psychi-atry* 135: 7-14.

Steinhauer. (2001). A New York Vastly Altered by AIDS. *New York Times,* June 4. http://nyt.com.

Stewart, B. (1997). Final Days at Home. *New York Times.* March 23. http://nyt.com.

Stoddard, S. (1992) *The Hospice Movement.* New York, NY: Vintage Books.

Stolberg, S. (1998) As Life Ebbs, So Does Time to Elect the Comfort of Hospice. *New York Times,* March 4. http://nyt.com.

Symborska, W. (1995). Nothing's a Gift, *A View With a Grain of Sand: Selected Poems.* New York, NY: Harcourt, Brace & Co.

Tasman, A. (1982). Loss of Self-Cohesion in Terminal Illness. *Journal of the American Academy of Psychoanalysis* 10: 515-526.

Thiermann, S. (1991). *If I Should Die Before I Wake: An Investigation of Nontraditional Spiritual Approaches to Working With the Dying (Hospice)* (doctoral dissertation). PA: Temple University. DAI 52: 3587.

Trauma, Dissociation and Loss Conference: First International. (1995). Crystal City, VA, Feb.

Van der Kolk, B., McFarland and Weisaeth, Eds. (1996). *Traumatic Stress: The Effects of Overwhelming Experience on Mind, Body and Society.* New York, NY: The Guilford Press.

Von Franz, M. L. (1986). *On Dreams and Death: A Jungian Interpretation.* Boston, MA: Shambala Pr.

Welman, M. (2000). Thanatos and Existance: Towards a Jungian Phenomenology of the Death Instinct. *Pathways Into the Jungian World: Phenomenology and Analytic Psychology.* Roger Brooke, Ed. Florence, KY: Taylor and Francis/Routledge.

Wheelwright, J. H. in collaboration with Haas, E., McClintock B., and Blodgett, A. (1981). *The Death of a Woman: How a Life Became Complete.* New York, NY: St. Martin's Press.

Whitmont, E. (1969). *The Symbolic Quest.* New York, NY: G.P. Putnam's Sons.

Whyte, D. (2012). The Well of Grief, *River Flow: New and Selected Poems,* Langley, Washington: Many Rivers Press.

Wilhelm, R. and Baynes, C., Trans. (1950). *I Ching or the Book of Changes.* New York, NY: Pantheon Books.

Wilhelm, R. and Jung, C. G. (1931). *The Secret of the Golden Flower: A Chinese Book of Life.* New York, NY: Harcourt, Brace & World.

Wilkes, P. (1997). Dying Well is the Best Revenge. *New York Times.* July 6. http://nyt.com.

Williams, Y. (1999). *The Art of Dying: A Jungian View of Patients' Drawings.* Springfield, IL: Charles Thomas.

Winnicott, D. (1958). *Through Paediatrics to Psycho-Analysis.* London, UK: Hogarth Press.

Winnicott, D. (1958). The Capacity to Be Alone. *International Journal of Psycho-Analysis* 39: 416-420.

Woodman, M. (1997). *Dancing in the Flames.* Boston, MA: Shambala Press.

_____. (2001). *Bone.* New York, NY and London, UK: Penguin Press.

Wright, S., et al. (2015). Meaning Centered Dream Work: A Pilot Study. *Palliative and Support Care,* Vol. 13:5, 1193-1211.

Young, W. (1960). Death of a Patient During Psychotherapy. *Psychiatry: Journal for the Study of Interpersonal Processes,* 23: 103-8.

Zender, J. (1986). *Dreams of Terminally Ill Patients in Relation to Levels of Depression and Death Anxiety (Cancer Content)* (doctoral dissertation). Michigan: University of Detroit. DAI 47:3977.

Zuehlke, T. and Watkins, J. (1975). The Use of Psychotherapy with Dying Patients: An Exploratory Study. *Journal of Clinical Psychology* 13(4): 729-732.

MOTION PICTURES, TELEVISION, AND AUDIO

Ashby, H. (Dir.), Higgins, G. and Mulvehill, (Prod.). (1971). *Harold and Maude.* (Motion Picture). California: Paramount.

Brooks, J. (Dir. and Prod.) (1983). *Terms of Endearment.* (Motion Picture). California: Paramount.

Halifax, J. (1997). *Being With Dying.* Audio Tapes. Boulder, CO: Sounds True.

Hiller, A. (Dir.) Minsky, H. (Prod.) (1970) *Love Story.* (Motion Picture). California: Paramount.

Kubrick, S. (Producer and Director). (1968). *2001: A Space Odyssey.* (Motion Picture). California, USA: Metro-Goldwyn-Mayer (MGM).

Mineola, A., Dir., Cooper, R., Prod. (1991*) Truly, Madly, Deeply.* (Motion Picture). UK: MGM.

Moyers, B. (2000). "On Our Own Terms: Moyers on Dying." Television Program. PBS/*Thirteen*/WNET New York.

Shadyac, T. (Dir.) Ferral, M. and Kemp, B. et al (Prod.) (1998) *Patch Adams.* (Motion Picture). California: Universal.

Thorpe, R. (Dir.)(1939). *Wizard of Oz.* (Motion Picture). California, Metro-Goldwyn-Mayer.

Ward, V. (Dir. and Prod.) (1998). *What Dreams May Come* (Motion Picture) California: Universal.

Wójtowicz-Vosloo, H. (Dir.) Perkins, B. (Prod.) (1998). *After Life.* (Motion Picture). New York: New Yorker Films.

Zucker, J. (Dir.) (1990). *Ghost.* (Motion Picture) California: Paramount.

ABOUT THE AUTHOR

Penelope Tarasuk, born in Washington, D.C., is a Jungian analyst in private practice in South Deerfield and Cambridge, Massachusetts. She is a senior training analyst with the New England Society of Jungian Analysts, C.G. Jung Institute of Boston, a member of the International Association of Analytic Psychology, served as an analyst and faculty member with the New Mexico Society of Jungian Analysts, Santa Fe, and is a current board member of Western MA Jung Association, Northampton, MA.

She attended the Philadelphia Museum College of Art and University of Maryland, College Park, MD and Seoul, South Korea. The Family Institute of Cambridge, MA. She has worked in human service for fifty years serving a wide range of patients and in many settings: in-patient hospital, UMD Counseling Center and the HELP Center: Drug Abuse, Crisis Intervention and Suicide Prevention service, community mental health agencies, director of a street clinic, and clinician in a residential adolescent drug treatment program in Lawrence, MA, and adult residential treatment in Santa Fe, NM. She provided consultation in Humane Education, Violence and Trauma for the Santa Fe Animal Shelter and Human Society. She works with individuals, couples, and families and has facilitated many groups, including an ongoing dream group in Santa Fe, NM that met consecutively for eleven years. She teaches and facilitates workshops across the US, in Mexico, and Greece on Jungian Psychology, Trauma, Breathwork, Dreaming Animals, and Creativity. She has maintained a private practice since 1988. She is an artist and is passionate about the importance of our relationship with nature.